THE NEW PRODUCTION OF
KNOWLEDGE

THE NEW PRODUCTION OF KNOWLEDGE

The Dynamics of Science and Research in Contemporary Societies

Michael Gibbons, Camille Limoges,
Helga Nowotny, Simon Schwartzman,
Peter Scott and Martin Trow

SAGE Publications
London • Thousand Oaks • New Delhi

© Forskningsråfdämnden (FRN) 1994
Box 6710
S-11385 Stockholm
Sweden

First published 1994
Reprinted 1995, 1996, 1997, 1999, 2000, 2002, 2004, 2005

SAGE Publications Ltd
1 Oliver's Yard, 55 City Road
London EC1Y 1SP

SAGE Publications Inc
2455 Teller Road
Thousand Oaks, California 91320

SAGE Publications India Pvt Ltd
B-42, Panchsheel Enclave
PO Box 4109
New Delhi-100 017

British Library Cataloguing in Publication Data

Gibbons, Michael
New Production of Knowledge: Dynamics of Science and
Research in Contemporary Societies
I. Title
303.483

ISBN 0-8039-7793-X
ISBN 0-8039-7794-8 (pbk)

Library of Congress catalog card number 94-066859

Typeset by M Rules
Printed and bound in Great Britain by
Biddles Ltd., King's Lynn, Norfolk

Contents

Preface

The volume here presented is the fruit of a sustained collaborative effort extending over several years. Our aim was to produce a book – an integrated text, rather than a series of chapters – devoted to exploring major changes in the way knowledge is being produced. The scope of our enquiry was to investigate these changes not only in science and technology but in the social sciences and the humanities as well, though in the end more pages have been devoted to the former than the latter. The organising principle of this work is that a new form of knowledge production is emerging alongside the traditional, familiar one. A new mode of knowledge production affects not only what knowledge is produced but also how it is produced; the context in which it is pursued, the way it is organised, the reward systems it utilises and the mechanisms that control the quality of that which is produced. These social characteristics of knowledge production have been well articulated in the case of disciplinary sciences, physics, chemistry and biology, for example, and we took them as paradigmatic of sound knowledge production in the sciences. To the extent that social sciences and the humanities have tried to imitate the physical sciences, similar social systems have been put in place to govern the production of knowledge in these areas as well.

To help in the description of the changes observed we have distinguished the new mode – Mode 2 – from the more familiar mode – Mode 1. Our view is that while Mode 2 may not be replacing Mode 1, Mode 2 is different from Mode 1 – in nearly every respect. The new mode operates within a context of application in that problems are not set within a disciplinary framework. It is transdisciplinary rather than mono- or multi-disciplinary. It is carried out in non-hierarchical, heterogeneously organised forms which are essentially transient. It is not being institutionalised primarily within university structures. Mode 2 involves the close interaction of many actors throughout the process of knowledge production and this means that knowledge production is becoming more socially accountable. One consequence of these changes is that Mode 2 makes use of a wider range of criteria in judging quality control. Overall, the process of knowledge production is becoming more reflexive and affects at the deepest levels what shall count as 'good science'.

It became clear, as the project progressed, that some of the ideas contained in Mode 2, were already present in the work of others. We acknowledge this and hope that the framework of analysis presented here will help to bring together the many insights on the social transformation of knowledge production that are currently embodied in the literature. The evidence that a new mode is emerging is, we believe, abundant but it is widespread. It is in the nature of Mode 2 that it manifests itself in a variety of different forms. It would have taken a major research programme – far beyond the resources at our disposal – to collect the appropriate data and establish precisely the limits of our hypothesis across the whole gamut of knowledge production. Rather than attempt this at this stage, we have tried to specify the new mode and its principal characteristics and to show how they are affecting knowledge production in science and industry and to some extent the social sciences and the humanities, and to try to indicate the imperatives of the new mode of knowledge production for policy. To this end, we have adopted an essay style of exposition. We have tried to raise some fundamental issues and, on occasion, to be provocative. Our purpose has been to stimulate discussion and debate, not bring it to an end. Clearly, this is a tall order and the reader will have to judge for him/herself the extent to which we have achieved any of these objectives. Whatever the verdict, we believe that the characteristics of Mode 2 developed in the text provide a useful heuristic for those seeking to understand what is changing in the sciences and what this implies for the future of our principal knowledge producing institutions.

Many organisations and individuals have been involved in the production of this volume. The first was the FRN, the Swedish Council for Research and Planning in Stockholm which conceived the project and funded it over three years. It was FRN, and in particular Roger Svensson, who guided the project through its early stages and who helped to select the team and set the style of work. The main work was done between 1990 and 1993. During the first two years, the project was defined and initial drafts of position papers prepared by members of the group. The initial task of drawing these papers into an integrated text was done during the third year while one of us (MG) was on sabbatical at the Centre for Higher Education Studies at the University of California, Berkeley. Subsequently, we have met in several collaborative sessions and worked line by line through the draft to produce the final text. This was truly great fun and gave us, first hand, some experience of working in Mode 2. However, we cannot let the reader imagine that the task was an easy one. It is always difficult to synthesise perspectives, not least for our administrative secretary Sue Alexander of the Science Policy Research Unit who showed remarkable aptitude in reducing the sometimes divergent thoughts of six scholars to an acceptable form of grammatical English on which we could all agree.

As academic coordinator, I have many people to thank for the part they have played in the gestation of this book. First, my co-authors. All distinguished scholars in their own right they none the less put up with my 'management style' in trying to shape the volume. Second, I would like to thank the University of Manchester for generously allowing me to take a sabbatical in 1992. Without this period, free from most of the cares of academic life, I doubt very much whether the first draft of an integrated text would have been produced so quickly. Third, I would like to thank Sheldon Rothblatt, Director of the Center for Higher Education Studies at the University of California, Berkeley and his staff Janet Ruyle and Pat Paulson who created the ideal conditions for work while I was in California. Fourth, I owe a great debt to the Economic and Social Science Research Council in the United Kingdom which through the Science Policy Support Group's programme on the 'Changing Relationship between Public Sector Science and Industry' provided the first insights into what was to become Mode 2. Fifth, we acknowledge our gratitude to Dr Brian Balmer who prepared the bibliography, glossary and references, and to Sue Alexander who coordinated the whole process of production through its final stages.

On a personal note, my special thanks to Justin and Joanna who, despite their youth, seem to have an intuitive understanding of the demands of scholarship and who patiently bore my long absences from home and even longer periods of preoccupation when I was actually there. And, finally my wife Gillian for, . . . well everything.

Michael Gibbons

Introduction

This volume is devoted to exploring changes in the mode of knowledge production in contemporary society. Its scope is broad, concerned with the social sciences and the humanities as well as with science and technology, though fewer pages are given to the former than to the latter. A number of attributes have been identified which suggest that the way in which knowledge is being produced is beginning to change. To the extent that these attributes occur across a wide range of scientific and scholarly activity, and persist through time they may be said to constitute trends in the way knowledge is produced. No judgement is made as to the value of these trends – that is, whether they are good and to be encouraged, or bad and resisted – but it does appear that they occur most frequently in those areas which currently define the frontier and among those who are regarded as leaders in their various fields. Insofar as the evidence seems to say that most of the advances in science have been made by 5 per cent of the population of practising scientists, these trends, because they seem to involve the intellectual leaders, probably ought not to be ignored.

It is the thesis of this book that these trends do amount, not singly but in their interaction and combination, to a transformation in the mode of knowledge production. The nature of this transformation is elaborated for science, in Chapter 1; for technology in Chapter 2; in Chapter 4 for the humanities; and for the social sciences throughout the text. The transformation is described in terms of the emergence alongside traditional modes of knowledge production that we will call Mode 2. By contrast with traditional knowledge, which we will call Mode 1, generated within a disciplinary, primarily cognitive, context, Mode 2 knowledge is created in broader, transdisciplinary social and economic contexts. The aim of introducing the two modes is essentially heuristic in that they clarify the similarities and differences between the attributes of each and help us understand and explain trends that can be observed in all modern societies. The emergence of Mode 2, we believe, is profound and calls into question the adequacy of familiar knowledge producing institutions, whether universities, government research establishments, or corporate laboratories.

Before discussing the attributes of Mode 2 and how they differ from Mode 1, it is necessary to call attention to a difficulty that is inherent in any attempt to describe a new mode of knowledge production. To the extent that a particular way of producing knowledge is dominant, all other claims will be judged with reference to it. In the extreme case, nothing recognisable as knowledge can be produced outside of the socially dominant form. This was the situation that confronted the early practitioners of the 'new' science when they confronted the Aristotelian Peripatetics at the beginning of the Scientific Revolution. It seems to be a recurrent historical pattern that intellectual innovations are first described as misguided by those whose ideas are dominant, then ignored and, finally, taken over by original adversaries as their own invention. Part of the explanation of this phenomenon derives from the fact that it is necessary to begin by describing the characteristics of the new in terms of the old. A further difficulty may be expected when the new mode is growing out of the existing one as is the case here. While it is always desirable to be clear about the terms being used, it is not possible at this early stage when so much is in flux to distinguish the two modes unequivocally. This is not a serious weakness, however, for if the new mode became a permanent feature on the social landscape a new vocabulary would emerge to handle the situation. And, of course, afterwards one may wonder what all the fuss was about. Hopefully, a more felicitous term will eventually be found to describe Mode 2, but it is important to keep in mind that a new name has been chosen because conventional terms – such as applied science, technological research, or research and development – are inadequate.

The problem of language is particularly difficult when trying to describe the nature of Mode 2 in areas where natural science is involved. In Western cultures, particularly, the terms science and knowledge are often used interchangeably or combined to form scientific knowledge. In the early phases of the scientific revolutions it was important to distinguish scientific from non-scientific forms of knowledge. A history of knowledge production since the seventeenth century could be written in terms of the efforts of the proponents of previously non-scientific forms of knowledge production to gain recognition as scientific. In Western cultures to be involved in non-scientific knowledge production is to place oneself beyond the pale, so that there is, today, a distinct sense of social isolation associated with participation in a non-scientific activity. But, the term scientific in this context already implies a distinct form of knowledge production. Its ideal is Newtonian empirical and mathematical physics.

In this essay, the term Mode 1 refers to a form of knowledge production – a complex of ideas, methods, values, norms – that has grown up to control the diffusion of the Newtonian model to more and more fields of enquiry and ensure its compliance with what is considered sound scientific practice. Mode 1 is meant to summarise in a single phrase the cognitive and social norms which must be followed in the production, legitimation and diffusion of knowledge of this kind. For many, Mode 1 is identical with what is meant by science. Its cognitive and social norms determine what shall count as significant problems, who shall be allowed to practise science and what constitutes good science. Forms of practice which adhere to these rules are by definition scientific while those that violate them are not. It is partly for these reasons that whereas in Mode 1 it is conventional to speak of science and scientists it has been necessary to use the more general terms knowledge and practitioners when describing Mode 2. This is intended merely to highlight differences not to suggest that practitioners of Mode 2 are not behaving according to the norms of scientific method. It is our contention that there is sufficient empirical evidence to indicate that a distinct set of cognitive and social practices is beginning to emerge and these practices are different from those that govern Mode 1. The only question may be whether they are sufficiently different to require a new label or whether they can be regarded simply as developments that can be accommodated within existing practices. The final answer to this question depends partly on acquiring more data and partly on how Mode 1 adapts to changing conditions in the economic and political environment.

Changes in practice provide the empirical starting point of this enquiry. These changes appear in the natural and social sciences but also in the humanities. They can be described in terms of a number of attributes which when taken together have sufficient coherence to suggest the emergence of a new mode of knowledge production. Analytically the set of attributes is used to allow the differences between Mode 1 and Mode 2 to be specified with some clarity. To summarise using terms which will be explored more fully below; in Mode 1 problems are set and solved in a context governed by the, largely academic, interests of a specific community. By contrast, Mode 2 knowledge is carried out in a context of application. Mode 1 is disciplinary while Mode 2 is transdisciplinary. Mode 1 is characterised by homogeneity, Mode 2 by heterogeneity. Organisationally, Mode 1 is hierarchical and tends to preserve its form, while Mode 2 is more heterarchical and transient. Each employs a different type of quality control. In comparison with Mode 1, Mode 2 is more socially accountable and reflexive. It includes a wider, more temporary and heterogeneous set of practitioners, collaborating on a problem defined in a specific and localised context.

Some Attributes of Knowledge Production in Mode 2

Knowledge Produced in the Context of Application
The relevant contrast here is between problem solving which is carried out following the codes of practice relevant to a particular discipline and problem solving which is organised around a particular application. In the

former, the context is defined in relation to the cognitive and social norms that govern basic research or academic science. Latterly, this has tended to imply knowledge production carried out in the absence of some practical goal. In Mode 2, by contrast, knowledge results from a broader range of considerations. Such knowledge is intended to be useful to someone whether in industry or government, or society more generally and this imperative is present from the beginning. Knowledge is always produced under an aspect of continuous negotiation and it will not be produced unless and until the interests of the various actors are included. Such is the context of application. Application, in this sense is not product development carried out for industry and the processes or markets that operate to determine what knowledge is produced are much broader than is normally implied when one speaks about taking ideas to the marketplace. None the less, knowledge production in Mode 2 is the outcome of a process in which supply and demand factors can be said to operate, but the sources of supply are increasingly diverse, as are the demands for differentiated forms of specialist knowledge. Such processes or markets specify what we mean by the context of application. Because they include much more than commercial considerations, it might be said that in Mode 2 science has gone beyond the market! Knowledge production becomes diffused throughout society. This is why we also speak of socially distributed knowledge.

Research carried out in the context of application might be said to characterise a number of disciplines in the applied sciences and engineering – for example, chemical engineering, aeronautical engineering or, more recently, computer science. Historically these sciences became established in universities but, strictly speaking, they cannot be called applied sciences, because it was precisely the lack of the relevant science that called them into being. They were genuinely new forms of knowledge though not necessarily of knowledge production because, they too, soon became the sites of disciplinary-based knowledge production in the style of Mode 1. These applied disciplines share with Mode 2 some aspects of the attribute of knowledge produced in the context of application. But, in Mode 2 the context is more complex. It is shaped by a more diverse set of intellectual and social demands than was the case in many applied sciences while it may give rise to genuine basic research.

Transdisciplinarity

Mode 2 does more than assemble a diverse range of specialists to work in teams on problems in a complex applications oriented environment. To qualify as a specific form of knowledge production it is essential that enquiry be guided by specifiable consensus as to appropriate cognitive and social practice. In Mode 2, the consensus is conditioned by the context of application and evolves with it. The determinants of a potential solution involve the integration of different skills in a framework of action but the consensus may be only temporary depending on how well it conforms to the requirements set by the specific context of application. In Mode 2 the shape of the final solution will normally be beyond that of any single contributing discipline. It will be transdisciplinary.

Transdisciplinarity has four distinct features. First, it develops a distinct but evolving framework to guide problem solving efforts. This is generated and sustained in the context of application and not developed first and then applied to that context later by a different group of practitioners. The solution does not arise solely, or even mainly, from the application of knowledge that already exists. Although elements of existing knowledge must have entered into it, genuine creativity is involved and the theoretical consensus, once attained cannot easily be reduced to disciplinary parts.

Second, because the solution comprises both empirical and theoretical components it is undeniably a contribution to knowledge, though not necessarily disciplinary knowledge. Though it has emerged from a particular context of application, transdisciplinary knowledge develops its own distinct theoretical structures, research methods and modes of practice, though they may not be located on the prevailing disciplinary map. The effort is cumulative, though the direction of accumulation may travel in a number of different directions after a major problem has been solved.

Third, unlike Mode 1 where results are communicated through institutional channels, the results are communicated to those who have participated in the course of that participation and so, in a sense, the diffusion of the results is initially accomplished in the process of their production. Subsequent diffusion occurs primarily as the original practitioners move to new problem contexts rather than through reporting results in professional journals or at conferences. Even though problem contexts are transient, and problem solvers highly mobile, communication networks tend to persist and the knowledge contained in them is available to enter into further configurations.

Fourth, transdisciplinarity is dynamic. It is problem solving capability on the move. A particular solution can become the cognitive site from which further advances can be made, but where this knowledge will be used next and how it will develop are as difficult to predict as are the possible applications that might arise from discipline-based research. Mode 2 is marked especially but not exclusively by the ever closer interaction of knowledge production with a succession of problem contexts. As with discoveries in Mode 1 one discovery may build upon another but in Mode 2, the discoveries lie outside the confines of any particular discipline and practitioners need not return to it for validation. New knowledge produced in this way may not fit easily into any one of the disciplines that contributed to the solution. Nor may it be easily referred to particular disciplinary institutions or recorded as disciplinary contributions. In Mode

2, communications in ever new configurations are crucial. Communication links are maintained partly through formal and partly through informal channels.

Heterogeneity and Organisational Diversity

Mode 2 knowledge production is heterogeneous in terms of the skills and experience people bring to it. The composition of a problem solving team changes over time as requirements evolve. This is not planned or coordinated by any central body. As with Mode 1, challenging problems emerge, if not randomly, then in a way which makes their anticipation very difficult. Accordingly, it is marked by:

1   An increase in the number of potential sites where knowledge can be created; no longer only universities and colleges, but non-university institutes, research centres, government agencies, industrial laboratories, think-tanks, consultancies, in their interaction.

2   The linking together of sites in a variety of ways – electronically, organisationally, socially, informally – through functioning networks of communication.

3   The simultaneous differentiation, at these sites, of fields and areas of study into finer and finer specialities. The recombination and reconfiguration of these subfields form the bases for new forms of useful knowledge. Over time, knowledge production moves increasingly away from traditional disciplinary activity into new societal contexts.

In Mode 2, flexibility and response time are the crucial factors and because of this the types of organisations used to tackle these problems may vary greatly. New forms of organisation have emerged to accommodate the changing and transitory nature of the problems Mode 2 addresses. Characteristically, in Mode 2 research groups are less firmly institutionalised; people come together in temporary work teams and networks which dissolve when a problem is solved or redefined. Members may then reassemble in different groups involving different people, often in different loci, around different problems. The experience gathered in this process creates a competence which becomes highly valued and which is transferred to new contexts. Though problems may be transient and groups short-lived, the organisation and communication pattern persists as a matrix from which further groups and networks, dedicated to different problems, will be formed. Mode 2 knowledge is thus created in a great variety of organisations and institutions, including multinational firms, network firms, small hi-tech firms based on a particular technology, government institutions, research universities, laboratories and institutes as well as national and international research programmes. In such environments the patterns of funding exhibit a similar diversity, being assembled from a variety of organisations with a diverse range of requirements and expectations which, in turn, enter into the context of application.

Social Accountability and Reflexivity

In recent years, growing public concern about issues to do with the environment, health, communications, privacy and procreation, and so forth, have had the effect of stimulating the growth of knowledge production in Mode 2. Growing awareness about the variety of ways in which advances in science and technology can affect the public interest has increased the number of groups that wish to influence the outcome of the research process. This is reflected in the varied composition of the research teams. Social scientists work alongside natural scientists, engineers, lawyers and businesspeople because the nature of the problems requires it. Social accountability permeates the whole knowledge production process. It is reflected not only in interpretation and diffusion of results but also in the definition of the problem and the setting of research priorities. An expanding number of interest, and so-called concerned, groups are demanding representation in the setting of the policy agenda as well as in the subsequent decision making process. In Mode 2 sensitivity to the impact of the research is built in from the start. It forms part of the context of application.

Contrary to what one might expect, working in the context of application increases the sensitivity of scientists and technologists to the broader implications of what they are doing. Operating in Mode 2 makes all participants more reflexive. This is because the issue on which research is based cannot be answered in scientific and technical terms alone. The research towards the resolution of these types of problem has to incorporate options for the implementation of the solutions and these are bound to touch the values and preferences of different individuals and groups that have been seen as traditionally outside of the scientific and technological system. They can now become active agents in the definition and solution of problems as well as in the evaluation of performance. This is expressed partly in terms of the need for greater social accountability, but it also means that the individuals themselves cannot function effectively without reflecting – trying to operate from the standpoint of – all the actors involved. The deepening of understanding that this brings, in turn, has an effect on what is considered worthwhile doing and, hence, on the structure of the research itself. Reflection of the values implied in human aspirations and projects has been a traditional concern of the humanities. As reflexivity within the research process spreads, the humanities too are experiencing an increase in demand for the sorts of knowledge they have to offer.

Traditionally, this has been the function of the humanities, but over the years the supply side – departments of philosophy, anthropology, history –

of such reflexivity has become disconnected from the demand side – that is from businesspeople, engineers, doctors, regulatory agencies and the larger public who need practical or ethical guidance on a vast range of issues (for example, pressures on the traditional humanities for culturally sensitive scenarios, and on legal studies for an empirically grounded ethics, the construction of ethnic histories, and the analysis of gender issues).

Quality Control

Criteria to assess the quality of the work and the teams that carry out research in Mode 2 differ from those of more traditional, disciplinary science. Quality in Mode 1 is determined essentially through the peer review judgements about the contributions made by individuals. Control is maintained by careful selection of those judged competent to act as peers which is in part determined by their previous contributions to their discipline. So, the peer review process is one in which quality and control mutually re-enforce one another. It has both cognitive and social dimensions, in that there is professional control over what problems and techniques are deemed important to work on as well as who is qualified to pursue their solution. In disciplinary science, peer review operates to channel individuals to work on problems judged to be central to the advance of the discipline. These problems are defined largely in terms of criteria which reflect the intellectual interests and preoccupations of the discipline and its gatekeepers.

In Mode 2 additional criteria are added through the context of application which now incorporates a diverse range of intellectual interests as well as other social, economic or political ones. To the criterion of intellectual interest and its interaction, further questions are posed, such as 'Will the solution, if found, be competitive in the market?' 'Will it be cost effective?', 'Will it be socially acceptable?' Quality is determined by a wider set of criteria which reflects the broadening social composition of the review system. This implies that 'good science' is more difficult to determine. Since it is no longer limited strictly to the judgements of disciplinary peers, the fear is that control will be weaker and result in lower quality work. Although the quality control process in Mode 2 is more broadly based, it does not follow that because a wider range of expertise is brought to bear on a problem that it will necessarily be of lower quality. It is of a more composite, multidimensional kind.

The Coherence of Mode 2

These attributes, while not present in every instance of Mode 2, do when they appear together have a coherence which gives recognisable cognitive and organisational stability to the mode of production. Just as in Mode 1 cognitive and social norms are adjusted to one another and produce disciplinary knowledge, so in Mode 2 new norms are emerging that are appropriate to transdisciplinary knowledge. In all kinds of knowledge production, individual and collective creativity find themselves in a varying relationship of tension and balance. In Mode 1 individual creativity is emphasised as the driving force of development and quality control operating through disciplinary structures organised to identify and enhance it, while the collective side, including its control aspects, is hidden under the consensual figure of the scientific community. In Mode 2 creativity is mainly manifest as a group phenomenon, with the individual's contribution seemingly subsumed as part of the process and quality control being exercised as a socially extended process which accommodates many interests in a given application process. Just as in Mode 1 knowledge was accumulated through the professionalisation of specialisation largely institutionalised in universities, so in Mode 2 knowledge is accumulated through the repeated configuration of human resources in flexible, essentially transient forms of organisation. The loop from the context of application through transdisciplinarity, heterogeneity, organisational diversity is closed by new adaptive and contextual forms of quality control. The result is a more socially accountable and reflexive mode of science. Many examples of these phenomena could be drawn from the biomedical and environmental sciences.

Although Mode 1 and Mode 2 are distinct modes of production, they interact with one another. Specialists trained in the disciplinary sciences do enter Mode 2 knowledge production. While some may return to their original disciplinary base others will choose to follow a trail of complex solving problems that are set by a sequence of application contexts. Conversely, some outputs of transdisciplinary knowledge production, particularly new instruments may enter into and fertilise any number of disciplinary sciences. Because of such interactions, there may be a temptation to reduce the new form to more familiar ones, to collapse Mode 2 into Mode 1, and thereby to minimise the significance of the changes outlined above. Though Mode 2 knowledge production interacts with Mode 1 it is different from it. Terms in common usage such as pre-competitive research, strategic research, mission-oriented research, applied research or industrial research and development still carry many of the social preconceptions of the function of disciplinary science; in particular, the idea that disciplinary science provides the inexhaustible well for future applications. The deeply held belief that if the disciplines do not flourish then fundamental insights will be missed, or that foundational theoretical knowledge cannot be produced and sustained outside of disciplinary structures may account for the persistence of the linear model of innovation in policy debates. Yet, it is increasingly the case in computer, materials, biomedical and environmental sciences that theories are developed in the context of application and that these continue to fertilise lines of intellectual advance that lie outside disciplinary frameworks. In Mode 2 things are done differently and when enough things are done differently one is entitled to say that a new form has emerged.

The reasons why this new mode of production has emerged at the present time are not hard to find. In the first place, Mode 1 has been eminently successful. Scientists long ago discovered that the most effective way to achieve this was through a process of specialisation in the cognitive realm, of professionalisation in the social realm and institutionalisation of the political realm. This pattern has governed the diffusion of science from one area of activity to another and it has tended to treat harshly those who tried to circumvent its controls. The disciplinary structure of knowledge reflects the successful operation of this pattern of cognitive and social control. But over the years the number of graduates grounded in the ethos of research together with some specialist skill have been too large for them all to be absorbed within the disciplinary structure. Some of them have gone into government laboratories, others into industry, while others have established their own laboratories, think-tanks and consultancies. As a consequence, the number of sites where competent research can be carried out has increased. These constitute the intellectual resources for, and social underpinnings of, Mode 2. Seen from another perspective, one might also say that the creation of many new sites is an unintended result of the process of massification of education and research.

The development of rapid transportation, as well as information and communication technologies have created a capability which allows these sites to interact. Mode 2 is critically dependent upon the emerging computer and telecommunication technologies and will favour those who can afford them. The interactions among these sites of knowledge have set the stage for an explosion in the number of interconnections and possible configurations of knowledge and skill. The outcome can be described as a socially distributed knowledge production system. In this system communication increasingly takes place across existing institutional boundaries. The outcome is a web whose nodes are now strung out across the globe and whose connectivity grows daily. Not surprisingly when traditional scientists begin to participate in this they are perceived to weaken disciplinary loyalty and institutional control. But contexts of application are often the sites of challenging intellectual problems and involvement in Mode 2 allows access to these and promises close collaboration with experts from a wide range of backgrounds. For many this can be a very stimulating work environment. Mode 2 shows no particular inclination to become institutionalised in the conventional pattern. The established structure of science can be expected to be concerned about this and about how quality control will be assured in a socially distributed knowledge production system but it is now a fact of life. Mode 2 is a response to the needs of both science and society. It is irreversible. The problem is how to understand and manage it.

Some Implications of Mode 2

One aim of this book is to draw attention to the existence of a number of attributes associated with the new kind of production of knowledge, and to show that these attributes possess sufficient coherence to be called a new mode of production. We argue that as Mode 1 has become the mode of production characteristic of disciplinary research institutionalised largely in universities, so Mode 2 is characterised by transdisciplinarity and institutionalised in a more heterogeneous and flexible socially distributed system. Having outlined its main features we are now in a position to consider the implications of this development.

The massification of higher education and the appropriation, after the Second World War, by the universities of a distinct research function have produced increasing numbers of people familiar with the methods of research, many of whom are equipped with specialised knowledge and skills of various kinds. Massification is now a strongly entrenched phenomenon, it is international in scope and is unlikely ever to be reversed. On the supply side, the numbers of potential knowledge producers flowing out of higher education is increasing and will continue to do so.

However, this expansion of higher education has an implication that has so far been little examined. Not only are increasingly more people familiar with science and competent in its methods, but also many of these are engaged in activities which have a research dimension. They have brought their knowledge and skills to bear on a wide range of problems in contexts and situations often very remote from the universities where they were originally trained. Scientific and technological knowledge production are now pursued not only in universities but also in industry and government laboratories, in think-tanks, research institutions and consultancies, etc. The expansion of higher education, internationally, has meant that the numbers of potential sites where recognisably competent research is being performed have increased. The implication, not yet fully grasped, is that to the extent that universities continue to produce quality graduates, they undermine their monopoly as knowledge producers. Many graduates have subsequently become competent to pass judgement on university research and belong to organisations which might do the job just as well. Universities are coming to recognise that they are now only one type of player, albeit still a major one, in a vastly expanded knowledge production process.

In parallel with this vast expansion in supply has been the expansion of the demand for specialist knowledge of all kinds. The interaction of supply and demand for specialist knowledge has many characteristics of a market, but there are some crucial differences. The function of a market is to bring supply and demand into balance and establish the terms of exchange. Traditionally, markets are understood to establish the prices at which the supply and demand of particular commodities will be in equilibrium. A market is a mechanism for allocating resources – labour and capital – to the production of commodities. It works most effectively in cases for which there is already a clearly specified demand and for which the factors of production are available. But markets also have a dynamic component. They can call forth new commodities the demand for which barely exists or, conversely, they can stimulate demand for commodities whose features are as yet unclear. In dynamic markets supply and demand mutually articulate one another.

Knowledge plays a crucial role in many dynamic markets. It is an important source of created comparative advantage for both its producers and users of all kinds and not only in industry. In some of these markets the terms of trade are more complex than may be indicated by comparative levels of costs and prices, and the medium of exchange more subtle than money. For example, in those markets which articulate the supply and demand for knowledge about the environment, there are many different kinds of exchanges among the many participants but the medium is a more complex blend of individual and social values than could be captured by monetary values alone. Because comparative advantage cannot be reduced to economic criteria such markets may be described rather as social than commercial markets but they are markets none the less. Within such markets, the sources of demand are manifold. They come from society in the form of public enquiries of various kinds, from governments in regard to a wide range of issues such as the adverse consequences of high risk technologies, and from a whole spectrum of institutions, interest groups and individuals who need to know more about particular matters. This complex set of actors form hybrid fora which provide stimuli for both the supply and demand of specialised knowledge. Both theoretical and practical knowledge are generated in these fora.

The requirement of industry for knowledge, particularly for the results of scientific and technological research, is widely appreciated. The expansion of demand for a flow of specialist knowledge among firms is perhaps less well understood. Specialist knowledge is often a key factor in determining a firm's comparative advantage. As the pressures of international competition increase firms have tried to meet the challenges presented through the introduction of new technologies. New technology is a necessary but not sufficient condition for successful innovative performance and increasingly, technological innovation depends upon using specialised knowledge to develop technologies in directions dictated by competitive pressures. Specialist knowledge is used partly because it provides a constantly replenishable source of created comparative advantage and partly because it can be difficult to imitate, particularly by firms whose national culture does not yet support a well articulated science and technology infrastructure. Since, in many sectors these firms represent the spearhead of international competition, specialised knowledge is at a premium but its acquisition is difficult and often too expensive for individual firms to replicate entirely in-house. To meet this exigency firms have become involved in a complex array of collaborative arrangements involving universities, governments and other firms, sometimes from within the same sector. In each case supply and demand are mediated by a market mechanism, but, again, it is not, or need not be, a narrowly commercial one.

In these markets knowledge itself may be sought continuously, but more often than not it is not readily available to be bought or sold, off the shelf, like other commodities. It is increasingly generated in the market nexus itself. In producing specialised knowledge markets operate to configure human and physical resources in a particular context of application. As a consequence of intensifying competition, the number of these contexts is expanding but the contexts are also transient. Markets are dynamic. They set new problems more or less continuously and the sites of knowledge production and their associated networks of communication move on. Knowledge is produced by configuring human capital. However, unlike physical capital, human capital is potentially more malleable. Human resources can be configured again and again to generate new forms of specialised knowledge. The ability to do this lies at the heart of many economies of scope which are currently regarded as crucial to survival in the marketplace.

The core of our thesis is that the parallel expansion in the number of potential knowledge producers on the supply side and the expansion of the requirement of specialist knowledge on the demand side are creating the conditions for the emergence of a new mode of knowledge production. The new mode has implications for all the institutions whether universities, government research establishments, or industrial laboratories that have a stake in the production of knowledge. The emergence of markets for specialised knowledge means that for each set of institutions the game is changing though not necessarily in the same way or at the same speed. There is no imperative for all institutions to adopt the norms and values of the new mode of knowledge production. Some firms and universities are already a long way along the path of change and this is manifested in the types of staff they recruit and in the complex range of collaborative agreements that they enter. However, the institutional goals to be achieved, the rules governing professional development and the social and technical determinants of competence will all need to be modified to the extent that the new mode of production becomes established.

The new mode – Mode 2 – is emerging alongside the traditional disciplinary structure of science and technology – Mode 1. Indeed, it is an outgrowth of it. In order to make clear what is involved in the new mode of production, the attributes of Mode 2 have been contrasted with those of Mode 1. From this analysis it will be clear that Mode 2 is not supplanting but rather is supplementing Mode 1. Mode 2 constitutes a distinct mode with its own set of cognitive and social norms. Some of these contrast sharply with deeply held beliefs about how reliable theoretical and practical knowledge should be generated but they should not for that reason be regarded as either superior or inferior to those operating in Mode 1. They are simply different. To some extent, however, the way in which Mode 2 becomes established in a particular context will be determined by the degree to which Mode 1 institutions wish to adapt themselves to the new situation.

The emergence of a socially distributed knowledge production system means that this type of knowledge is both supplied by and distributed to individuals and groups across the social spectrum. Communications at institutional levels tend to be bypassed because of the need for rapid, flexible responses to problems. Although one may expect variety in the extent that Mode 2 becomes dominant, it is a correlate to the socially distributed knowledge production system which is now emerging. To the extent that institutions become permeable, then Mode 2 can operate. The degree to which current knowledge producing institutions become more permeable will not alter the fundamental fact that knowledge production is becoming more widely distributed; that is, it takes place in many more types of social settings; that it is no longer concentrated in a relatively few institutions, and involves many different types of individuals and organisations in a vast array of different relationships. Such behaviour will simply cause other linkages to become established which in the end may leave them scientifically and technically isolated from some intellectual developments.

Socially distributed knowledge production is tending towards the form of a global web whose numbers of inter-connections are being continuously expanded by the creation of new sites of production. As a consequence, in Mode 2 communications are crucial. At present this is maintained partly through formal collaborative agreements and strategic alliances and partly through informal networks backed up by rapid transportation and electronic communications. But this is only the tip of the iceberg. To function the new mode needs to be supported by the latest that telecommunications and computer technologies have to offer. Mode 2, then, is both a cause and a consumer of innovations which enhance the flow and transformation of information.

It is one of the imperatives of Mode 2 that exploitation of knowledge requires participation in its generation. In socially distributed knowledge production the organisation of that participation becomes the crucial factor. The goals of participation are no longer simply to secure some national advantage, commercial or otherwise. Indeed, the very notion of what constitutes an economic benefit, and for whom, is at the root of many debates not only in environmental science but in biotechnology and the medical sciences as well. For example, the current push towards 'clean' technologies is about more than just economic benefit. It is also about stabilising collapsing ecological systems, the health and well being of populations as well as commercial gain. This is to say that although Mode 2 is exemplified in this book only in relation to knowledge production, it has co-evolutionary effects in other areas, for example in economics, the prevailing division of labour, and the sense of community.

The appearance of Mode 2 is creating new challenges for governments. National institutions need to be de-centred – to be made more permeable – and governments through their policies can promote change in this direction. These policies will be more effective if, concurrently, they become more proactive brokers in a knowledge production game which includes, in addition to the interests and ambitions of other nations, the policies of supranational institutions, such as the European Union (EU). The effectiveness of governments' brokering abilities now underlies the competitiveness of their national innovation systems. This will be reflected both in their ability to participate in knowledge production that may be taking place anywhere in the world but also in their ingenuity in appropriating that knowledge with their innovation system.

Ingenuity is required because sooner or later collaboration must turn into competition. This is in the nature of the wealth creating process as it is presently constituted. Simply to monitor the interface between competition and collaboration would be a difficult enough task. To manage it to national advantage is a challenge that governments will neglect to their cost. As with scientists and technologists, governments, too, need to learn to operate in the context of application, and increasingly this involves supranational institutions. These have political, social and economic dimensions in the case of the EU in Western Europe, but more narrowly economic aims in the cases of the North American Free Trade Agreement (NAFTA) and the General Agreement on Tariffs and Trade (GATT). Key questions are whether supranational institutions can assist in this and how nations ought to position themselves relative to these larger systems.

It is perhaps ironic that it should fall to governments to punch holes in the very institutions that in an earlier day were established to maintain its science and technology capability. But along with many other apparently fixed notions, the purpose and function of these institutions need to be re-thought in the light of the emergence of Mode 2. This will reveal the need for a different approach to policy, particularly for the integration of education, science and technology and competition policy into a comprehensive innovation policy that is sensitive to the fact that knowledge production is socially distributed. In Europe, particularly, national policies that will enhance the potential of national institutions need to be developed in concert with those of the EU. The developing countries, too, need to take stock. For many of them, access will continue to be a problem not only because capability is lacking but also because governments there still model their scientific and technological institutions on assumptions that no longer apply to the kinds of scientific and technological activities on which their aspirations depend.

1
Evolution of Knowledge Production

Summary

In this chapter we begin by defining the distinctive characteristics of Mode 1 and Mode 2 knowledge production, emphasising that the latter has evolved out of the disciplinary matrix of the former and continues to exist alongside it. The new mode of knowledge production involves different mechanisms of generating knowledge and of communicating them, more actors who come from different disciplines and backgrounds, but above all different sites in which knowledge is being produced. The problems, projects or programmes on which practitioners temporarily focus constitute new sites of knowledge production which are moved into and take place more directly in the context of application or use. There is no pressure to institutionalise these activities in a permanent way or for participants to move permanently to a new institutional location. As a consequence, this dispersed and transient way of knowledge production leads to results which are also highly contextualised. Due to their inherent transdisciplinarity they greatly enhance further diffusion and production of new knowledge through techniques, instrumentation and the tacit knowledge which move to new contexts of application and use.

One of the characteristic features of Mode 2 is its transdisciplinarity. Another is what we call its social distribution, that is, the diffusion over a wide range of potential sites of knowledge production and different contexts of application or use. But the socially distributed nature of Mode 2 knowledge production is above all embodied in people and the ways they are interacting in socially organised forms. Hence, the emphasis on the tacit components of knowledge which we see as taking precedence over the codified components. While this leads to a gradual rapprochement of how knowledge production is organised in the academic cultures and in firms, the firm's business strategy in organising its specific technological dimension acquires all the more importance in choosing its design configuration.

A crucial consequence resulting from the shift in knowledge production from Mode 1 to Mode 2 bears upon quality control. Its mechanisms and the criteria upon which it is based are bound to range also over a wider and more differentiated area, both along an institutional and a cognitive–organisational dimension inherent in quality control mechanisms. In general we claim that quality control too becomes more context- and use-dependent. In a more dispersed institutional space, quality control also takes on more transient and temporary forms and fluid norms. But above all, success is defined differently in Mode 2. It includes additional criteria to the traditional one of scientific excellence, such as efficiency or usefulness which are defined in terms of the contributions the work has made to the overall solution of transdisciplinary problems. In other words, the environment of research already structured by application or use will have to be taken into account, making room for multiple criteria not only in general, but also in relation to specific expectations and results.

In order to understand the dynamics of Mode 2 knowledge production better we draw a distinction between homogeneous and heterogeneous growth. With heterogeneous growth we refer to a process of differentiation and diffusion through which rearrangement of component elements takes place within a given process or set of activities. The process of heterogeneous growth is captured by us in a conceptual framework which we call the model of increasing density of communication. We maintain that the origins of the stupendous heterogeneous growth which is exhibited by the science and technology systems can be located on three levels of communication: communication between science and society, communication among scientific practitioners, and, metaphorically speaking, communication with the entities of the physical and social world. On all these three levels as well as through their interlinkages, communication density has increased in a dramatic fashion with the inbuilt heterogeneity providing a powerful predictor for further heterogeneous growth and its societal distribution.

Finally, we draw attention to some specific features of innovative activities in science and technology which fall under a Mode 2 production display. They are based upon the recovery of interest in specific, ordered structures, rather than the search for first principles and the concomitant distributive role that techniques and instrumentation, practical skills and tacit knowledge come to play. The second feature is innovation based upon knowledge of and practice through design. The intention here is to use the improved understanding of specific ordered structures to build, manipulate and control their operation in specific conditions and, perhaps even more importantly, for specific functions and purposes. The third feature contributing to innovation under Mode 2 conditions is the role that computers and especially computational modelling have come to play, opening the way to develop both routines that are independent of particular applications and hence can be used to meet a wide variety of uses and of building more sophisticated techniques and instruments that will enhance the design principle and its range of application.

The production of knowledge is advancing into a new phase. It operates according to new imperatives in tension with the traditional way of doing things with far-reaching implications. These changes are described in this book in terms of a shift in emphasis from a Mode 1 to a Mode 2. The main attributes of Mode 2 have already been summarily described in the Introduction. Mode 1 is discipline-based and carries a distinction between what is fundamental and what is applied; this implies an operational distinction between a theoretical core and other areas of knowledge such as the engineering sciences, where the theoretical insights are translated into applications. By contrast, Mode 2 knowledge production is transdisciplinary. It is characterised by a constant flow back and forth between the fundamental and the applied, between the theoretical and the practical. Typically, discovery occurs in contexts where knowledge is developed for and put to use, while results – which would have been traditionally characterised as applied – fuel further theoretical advances. Discovery in the context of application in the case of hypersonic aircraft is illustrated in Box 1.1. Mode 2 is characterised by a shift away from the search for fundamental principles towards modes of enquiry oriented towards contextualised results. Further, the experimental process itself is increasingly being guided by the principles of design, originally developed in the industrial context. It is becoming possible to reverse the conventional procedures for making certain substances, such as molecules, chemicals and materials. For example, some materials can now be built up atom by atom, or molecule by molecule, by design, in order to obtain a product with specified properties. In this, the product and the process by which new materials are made become integrated in the design process, implying a closer integration of the process of discovery with that of fabrication.

Mode 2 creates a novel environment in which knowledge flows more easily across disciplinary boundaries, human resources are more mobile, and the organisation of research more open and flexible.

Box 1.1
Discovery in the context of application: the case of hypersonic aircraft

Some research programmes, although industrially-oriented, may deal with scientific and technological questions well beyond the current frontiers of knowledge and so suggest new problems and shape new research agendas. This situation is well illustrated in the search for a viable hypersonic aircraft now being undertaken by many nations.

Scientists have long contemplated the construction of an aircraft capable of attaining satellite speeds, taking off like a regular airplane and returning to earth once its mission is accomplished. The success of this project depends on solving the problem of propulsion generated by aerobic motors which use air as the combustant rather than an oxygen mass.

However, at hypersonic speeds beyond Mach 6 supersonic combustion becomes necessary, requiring the difficult merger of aerobic principles with hypersonic speed in the perfecting of a supersonic ramjet, scramjet. The production of a new vehicle is thought to require a change in technological paradigm. There is a belief that conventional aerobic propulsion systems cannot function at hypersonic speeds. Paradigmatic change implies discontinuities, scientific as well as technological. The two traditional supports for the elaboration of new technological concepts, science and the design experience of previous technological generations – the supersonic ramjet, in this case – can provide only certain, limited guidance. In the case of hypersonic technologies, the state of science does not yet permit the development of predictive models and therefore is of limited usefulness in the elaboration of designs and innovation.

Lack of direction from existing science. In the case of combustion at Mach 5 to 6, the first barrier to investigation is the near impossibility of producing experimentally, on the ground, the data necessary to predict the performance of the scramjet concept. There are no installations capable of reproducing the combination of speeds, pressures and temperatures necessary to simulate hypersonic flight. Wind tunnel experiment can only be of short duration – a few seconds. This weakness is partly overcome by mathematical simulation methods. Here, however, there are also immense difficulties. The solution of supersonic combustion equations would require very long calculation times. The simulations therefore comprise significant approximations. Another crucial problem is the absence of a predictive law for turbulence. Finally, simulations do not eliminate completely the need for tests on real vehicles. Calculations may none the less minimise the quantity of experimental work necessary. They enable researchers for example to limit wind tunnel tests to those precise areas where simulations are too difficult or do not provide sufficiently precise results. In the final analysis the current difficulty of ensuring synergy between calculations and real tests reveals that science is still far from being able to provide predictive models for innovation and analytical design.

Discontinuities with previous experience. A further problem is evident in results obtained at the threshold of Mach 5 many of which are no longer valid beyond Mach 5. Certain physical–chemical laws are even reversed once one passes from the supersonic domain to the hypersonic. Different concepts need to be developed for the different velocity regimes. There is therefore a discontinuity between supersonic and hypersonic domains which precludes evolutionary development based on modest additional investments in human and physical capital. In addition, the analogical links between aerobic propulsion and rocket propulsion are relatively insignificant. They do not allow for more than a small likelihood of transferring knowledge from one domain to the other.

In this situation of uncertainty the primary need is for information on the very structure of problems involved and to overcome a critical lack in the scientific data necessary for the operations of measurement, test, control and trial. New instruments, techniques and knowledge are required. Currently many hypersonic programmes' research are oriented towards the production of such an instrumental basis.

The point is that this research phase precedes basic and applied research and contains a strong technological dimension. The formulation of this research agenda itself cannot be understood without paying attention to prior developments in the realm of technology, particularly instrumentation technology. This will structure the context of application and set

future problems for scientists and engineers from many backgrounds.

Source: **Foray and Conesa (1993)**

Mode 2 is spreading across the entire landscape of science and technology. The proliferation of sites outside of normal disciplinary structures and institutions developed since the turn of the nineteenth century, in which recognisably competent research is taking place, opens up a vast field of interconnections. As interactions multiply, the epistemological status of the knowledge thus produced does not follow traditional, that is, disciplinary criteria. In Mode 1, any knowledge is validated by the sanction of a clearly defined community of specialists. In transdisciplinary Mode 2, such legitimating structures are either lacking or dysfunctional. Transdisciplinary research also needs some legitimating procedures, but they are different because different criteria are being applied to what is considered good research. Moreover, with the broadening and relatively transient character of the communities of practitioners involved the assessment of knowledge will occur through a much stronger societal contextualisation.

Science does not stand outside of society dispensing its gifts of knowledge and wisdom; neither is it an autonomous enclave that is now being crushed under the weight of narrowly commercial or political interests. On the contrary, science has always both shaped and been shaped by society in a process that is as complex as it is variegated; it is not static but dynamic. The range of possible problems which could be tackled by science is indefinitely large and therefore the research agenda cannot be understood in purely intellectual terms.

Science possesses a variegated internal structure, made of a vast number of communities or specialisms, each with distinct forms of practice and specific modes of internal and external communication. In fact, so diverse are the activities that comprise the scientific enterprise that it is perhaps misleading to group them under a common label. Contemporary science appears to be in more or less continuous flux, a state of turbulence which contrasts sharply with the perception of science as a socially autonomous enterprise with stable institutions, well delineated disciplinary structures and ageing slightly remote practitioners.

In Mode 1 disciplinary research, the term paradigm is used to denote a provisional consensus among the relevant set of practitioners. It is the result of a particular mode of organisation, and it denotes a way of seeing things, of defining and giving priority to certain problem sets. Many scientists are employed by universities, work within the structure of a particular specialism, and regularly teach within a disciplinary structure.

However, in that seemingly comfortable world they have had to evolve a wide range of strategies for survival. Personal research strategies have become necessary because the scientific enterprise has grown to such proportions that resources must be allocated to those who demonstrate continuous creativity. The more astute researchers in trying to balance their need for equipment and staff with the need to work within a given paradigmatic structure, build their careers around a broad base of research funding. They work on problems that are intellectually challenging and interesting enough to catch the attention of relevant peers and a range of funding agencies, and they try to establish their particular ideas, theories and methods as paradigmatic, that is, as the way to do things. By contrast, scientists who refuse to take a strategic approach to their careers face the prospect of being left behind as research councils, foundations and even universities adjust their resources to new horizons. Such scientists will be chronically short of research funds, become relatively unproductive and, in the end, come to be judged by their peers as mediocre performers. In this situation, the ability to raise funds becomes, in itself, an indicator of success.

By adopting a strategic approach to their careers, many scientists have become entrepreneurs and have had to loosen their disciplinary affiliations while contributing to the blurring of subject boundaries. Scientists have long appreciated that there is no intrinsic reason why the funding strategies of governments, firms, or foundations should conform to the current internal, cognitive structure of their discipline. Over the years, they have exercised great ingenuity in translating their own research interests into the language appropriate to other agendas. This has generated an awareness of problems beyond the immediate concerns of particular specialisms. Working in a problem context tends to improve appreciation of the importance of transdisciplinarity and also softens the distinctions between pure and applied science, between what is curiosity-oriented and what is mission-oriented research. The constant search for funds has indirectly increased the permeability of knowledge. To the extent that the imperatives of a problem context require cooperation or networking with other practitioners, whether in industrial, governmental or university laboratories, whether nationally or globally, the hold of established modes of knowledge production is weakened. In brief, much of the impulse for a shift to Mode 2 knowledge production has been endogenous to the practice of Mode 1.

All these changes are reflected in the ethos of the newest fields. The development of science has now reached a stage where many scientists have lost interest in the search for first principles. They believe that the natural world is too complex an entity to fall under a unitary description that is both comprehensive and useful, in the sense of being able to guide further research. In fields such as genetic engineering and biotechnology, information theory and information technology, artificial intelligence, microelectronics, advanced materials, researchers do not concern themselves with the basic principles of the world but with specific ordered structures within it (Barnes, 1985). The current upsurge of interest in applications is only partly a reflection of the persistence of commercial and military interests in science and technology. Equally important has been the shift of interest within science to the understanding of concrete systems and processes. This is reflected in the shift in emphasis from Mode 1 to Mode 2.

Though we have so far spoken mainly of science, the trend described obtains no less in technology. Indeed, the distinction between the two is becoming in most regards highly questionable. The idea that technology is also a form of knowledge is obscured by the tangibility of its artefacts. Artefacts are the outcome of a transformation process in which energy and matter in one form are transformed into energy and matter in another, often with better performance characteristics along some dimension. The aim of generating technology is to improve performance by rearranging existing elements. Though we are familiar with the outputs of various transformation processes, these artefacts often conceal their most basic constituents.

To concentrate on technology as artefact means keeping the lid very firmly on the 'black box' in which the transformation process occurs. It obscures the role of knowledge as a key element in this process. Only by opening the black box can the cognitive dimension of technology be unravelled. Certain commonalities in the ways in which scientific and technological knowledge are produced are then highlighted and the process by which science, technology and industry are being brought into closer contact is clarified.

Technology as a form of knowledge displays some of the traits of the paradigmatic structure of disciplinary science. Technological knowledge is a mixture of codified and tacit components. Codified knowledge need not be exclusively theoretical but it needs to be systematic enough to be written down and stored, whether in a computer database, a university library or in a research report. As such, it is available to anyone who knows where to look. Tacit knowledge, by contrast, is not available as a text and may conveniently be regarded as residing in the heads of those working on a particular transformation process, or to be embodied in a particular organisational context. The distinction between codified and tacit knowledge can be complemented by a parallel distinction between migratory and embedded knowledge. The former is mobile and can move rapidly across organisational boundaries, while the latter is less so because its movement is constrained in a given network or set of social relations. While some technological knowledge is codified and migratory, the majority of it is tacit and embedded, and for that reason is not generally available. It tends to move between and with individuals as they move from problem to problem and from one organisational context to another. Tacit knowledge is learned on the job through training and experience. In technological knowledge the tacit component may be larger than the codified one; although in a particular context it may be difficult to determine the relative importance.

Technological knowledge results from the decisions and actions taken by communities of practitioners. As in science, these communities identify the significant problems, develop methods to deal with them, supply model solutions to handle the day-to-day puzzles that emerge from following paradigmatic procedures.

Commercial applications are not usually developed in universities and government laboratories but in firms or business units though this is now changing. For our purposes a firm is different from either a university or a government laboratory in that it employs individuals who are 'practitioners' from a number of communities, be they scientific, technological or managerial. The job of management is to configure the competence of individuals into a distinct, firm-specific knowledge base which will form the core of its capability to compete in national and international markets. At the same time they continue to belong to a much wider set of communities on which the firm may be able to draw when it is faced with problems beyond the immediate range of expertise of its employees. Communication is eased because employees share with other members of these communities the same paradigms and are governed by the same basic principles of 'best practice'. The communal character can be limited, however, by secrecy and other restrictions that the privatisation of knowledge entails.

A firm's competence is more than the sum of the professional competence of its workforce. It also includes the more focused knowledge that bears upon the transformation process the firm is exploiting. That knowledge is organised in a way analogous to science and technology, but it is different in that it depends also on the firm's business strategy and its specific technological dimension. This strategic agenda defines a specific design configuration which the firm will try to exploit in the competitive arena. As with scientists and technologists, so businesspeople seek to establish in the marketplace their specific way of doing things. The choice of a design configuration commits the firms early on to a specific way of doing things and, by implication, to not exploring alternatives.

While many elements of a firm's knowledge base are codified and public, the specific elements which relate to its chosen design configuration are tacit and proprietary. Proprietary knowledge is codified and can be subject to licensing and commercialisation while tacit knowledge is implicit in the professional and institutional culture of a firm. Proprietary knowledge is protected by patents and trade secrecy and is usually perceived as typical of business firms and also of military establishments. Tacit knowledge is not exclusive to business firms since it is present in the research practices of any scientific and technological community. Contrary to what may appear to be the case, the competitive advantage of a firm lies less in its pool of proprietary knowledge than on its base of tacit competence. As proprietary knowledge is utilised it is subject to imitation, adaptation and replacement and gradually loses its market value. Tacit knowledge can only be acquired by hiring the people who possess it and it is the principal way a firm may replenish its basket of unique technologies.

The prevalence of tacit over proprietary knowledge brings the culture of technologically advanced firms much closer to academic cultures than is usually assumed. The isomorphism between these structures allows frequent interactions which lie at the root of the perception that science, technology and industry are moving closer together, and support our contention that interactions are increasingly taking place in the context of application. They share, in addition, a common behavioural pattern. Each is driven in part by a process of competition and in part by the need to collaborate. In science, competition is for academic recognition while in the technology system it is for technical efficiency, and in industry for that particular type of efficiency that generates a financial return. In each regime, individuals and teams try to establish as dominant their particular ways of doing things, their respective paradigms. Dominance depends on creativity which is a matter of skills, resources and organisation. Each operates in a regime where resources are limited and while success may relax this constraint, it will never entirely remove it. To some extent, this limitation can be met by collaboration. But more is involved in collaboration than the sharing of resources. As we shall see, the context of use is increasingly one where the best scientists and technologists meet and where they develop novel theoretical ideas and practical procedures.

The general significance of the shift from Mode 1 to Mode 2 for science and technology being so posited, we will outline in the remainder of this chapter two different sets of questions. First, we will address some of the major phenomenological aspects of Mode 2: its manner of producing knowledge in a transdisciplinary way, and the way quality control is exercised over the results of that production. Second, we will start to explore the dynamics of Mode 2 in terms of an increase in the heterogeneity of its constituents and of an increase in the density of the constitutive communication processes it exhibits with society, between scientific practitioners, and with the physical and social worlds. This increasing heterogeneity of constituents and of constitutive communications make explicit how socially distributed knowledge is at the core of Mode 2.

On the Phenomenology of the New Mode of Knowledge Production

Transdisciplinarity
Transdisciplinarity is the privileged form of knowledge production in Mode 2. It corresponds to a movement beyond disciplinary structures in the constitution of the intellectual agenda, in the manner in which resources are deployed, and in the ways in which research is organised, results communicated and the outcome evaluated. In that regard Mode 2 derives its impetus from a context which is totally different from the one which prevailed before the rise of specialised, disciplinary science in the nineteenth century when the scene might have been described as non-disciplinary. Mode 2 is evolving from a strongly disciplinarised context and as we have already stressed, knowledge produced under these conditions is characterised by aiming a use or action, that is towards 'application' in its broader sense.

In the production of transdisciplinary knowledge, the intellectual agenda is not set within a particular discipline, nor is it fixed by merely juxtaposing professional interests of particular specialists in some loose fashion leaving to others the task of integration at a later stage. Integration is not provided by disciplinary structures – in that regard the knowledge process is not interdisciplinary, it cuts across disciplines – but is envisaged and provided from the outset in the context of usage, or application in the broad sense specified earlier. Working in an application context creates pressures to draw upon a diverse array of knowledge resources and to configure them according to the problem in hand. The context of application is already intellectually structured, even if only in very general terms and provides heuristic guidelines. The search for a fundamental computer architecture is already a search for an architecture and not something else. Some participants may have a general idea of how the search should proceed and what knowledge and skills are required. There can, of course, be more than one view as to the best way to proceed and such divergences may fuel a process of competition. A brief description of the value of transdisciplinarity, and why it so often fails is given in Box 1.2.

Box 1.2
On transdisciplinarity

Why is transdisciplinarity valued so highly and why do so many efforts which are undertaken to establish it fail?

The problem with transdisciplinarity is the following: precisely because it so universally acclaimed as something positive, everyone believes it can be brought about just by aspiring to it. A closer look, however, reveals that much which is thought to be inter- or transdisciplinary in reality amounts to a mere accumulation of knowledge supplied from more than one discipline.

The yearning for inter- or transdisciplinarity and much of the rhetoric to which it is embedded is rooted in the nostalgia for an epoch when the 'unification of science' still appeared to be possible. In some fields, like physics, the 'dream of a final theory' is still very much alive (Weinberg, 1993). Such dreams reveal an understandable nostalgia for a pattern of knowledge production which is the exact opposite of what seemingly prevails today; the relentless increase in further specialisation of scientific knowledge and its diversification into ever more narrow areas. These processes and the speed with which they take place signal the breakdown of a common understanding across scientific disciplines, the loss of an intellectual common grasp for their development and the impossibility of communication across specialisms. Even among neighbouring specialities and among subfields within one discipline increasing difficulties are experienced in maintaining standards of expert scientific literacy. These tendencies are underlined by the proliferation of ever new scientific journals which explore more and more specialised intellectual market niches, increasing complicity in the classification systems of knowledge, a plethora of conferences, meetings and other signs which are the outward manifestation of the growth of the scientific technological labour force and its further specialisation and diversification.

The positive esteem accorded to inter- or transdisciplinarity is the expression of the wish to reinstate communality.

Since transdisciplinarity has become a value in its own right, it is often naively believed that striving for it is insufficient ground for achieving it. Experience, however, shows that numerous deliberate attempts to set it up, often with the best of intentions, were doomed to failure, unsuccessful projects are especially high when centred around university teaching.

There have been many attempts to discern pluri from inter- and transdisciplinarity. Following the definition given by Erich Jantsch (1972), pluri-/multidisciplinarity is characterised by the autonomy of the various disciplines and does not lead to changes in the existing disciplinary and theoretical structures. Cooperation consists in working on the common theme but under different disciplinary perspectives.

Interdisciplinarity is characterised by the explicit formulation of a uniform, discipline-transcending terminology or a common methodology. The form scientific cooperation takes consists in working on different themes, but within a common framework that is shared by the disciplines involved. Transdisciplinarity arises only if research is based upon a common theoretical understanding and must be accompanied by a mutual interpenetration of disciplinary epistemologies. Cooperation in this case leads to a clustering of disciplinary rooted problem-solving and creates a transdisciplinary homogenised theory or model pool.

In contrast to the widely held views and attempts that have been undertaken to set up transdisciplinarity by fist only, we do not argue for transdisciplinarity as a positive value per se. We see the emergence of a new mode of knowledge production as resulting from wider societal and cognitive pressures. It arises out of the existing dysfunctionalities and breakdowns of disciplinary modes of problem-solving. In the language of self-organisation, it emerges only once sufficient disturbances shake up the system of knowledge production. While it can be argued that the successful establishment of a particular field as transdisciplinary or, in the terminology of Erich Jantsch, as a clustering of disciplinary rooted problem-solving methods, is likely to mimic in the longer run the successful institutionalisation of a discipline, and hence becomes a discipline itself, our interest is in knowledge production as an ongoing process and the changes that occur in the ways how it is produced. A transdisciplinary mode consists in a continuous linking and relinking, in specific clusterings and configurations of knowledge which is brought together on a temporary basis in specific contexts of application. Thus, it is strongly oriented towards and driven by problem-solving. Its theoretical-methodological core, while cross-cutting through well-established disciplinary cores, is often locally driven and locally constituted, thus, any such core is highly sensitive to further local mutations depending on the context of application. The transdisciplinary mode of knowledge production described by us does not necessarily aim to establish itself as a new, transdisciplinary discipline, nor is it inspired by restoring cognitive unity. To the contrary, it is essentially a temporary configuration and thus highly mutable. It takes its particular shape and generates the content of

its theoretical and methodological core in response to prob-
lem-formulations that occur in highly specific and local
contexts of application. Just as the debate about nature and
nurture and about the adaptability of human culture to biological universals has moved beyond an 'either/or' answer
and focuses instead on specific modes of learning and cultural responses, so it is with scientific and technological
knowledge production: it is the specific mode that shapes
the outcome.

Still, the search within a context of application is not a haphazard affair.
Knowledge production will be guided by theoretical considerations as
well as by the limitation of experimental methods. And though it takes its
starting point from the intellectual frameworks of all those who participate
in the search, it soon leaves them behind to follow new paths. Over time
a new framework, a Mode 2 framework, will evolve – for example, the
basic architecture will be hit upon. It will be different from any of the constituent frameworks, yet could not have been developed without them.
The chosen Mode 2 framework will usually guide a great deal of further
work, but it might happen that all those involved will return to their original discipline while others will be recruited to take the process further.
The new Mode 2 framework constitutes a new point of departure from
which further problems will arise and if they are demanding enough, the
same or different individuals will be drawn to work on them. Disciplines
are no longer the only locus of the most interesting problems, nor are they
the homes to which scientists must return for recognition or rewards.
Over a lifetime these 'experts' may well stray a long way from their original disciplines, having worked in their careers on a wide array of
stimulating problems.

In transdisciplinary contexts, disciplinary boundaries, distinctions
between pure and applied research, and institutional differences between,
say, universities and industry, seem to be less and less relevant. Instead,
attention is focused primarily on the problem area, or the hot topic, pref-
erence given to collaborative rather than individual performance and
excellence judged by the ability of individuals to make a sustained contribution in open, flexible types of organisation in which they may only
work temporarily. None the less, a new mode of knowledge production
cannot simply force its way onto the institutional stage. A certain number
of basic conditions must be fulfilled if it is to become institutionalised.
The search for understanding must be guided by agreed models and sets
of experimental techniques, its articulation must follow the canons of
empirical method, its conclusions must be communicable to a wider
community and be repeatable by others. To qualify as such, knowledge

must form an organised stock and its methods of working must be transparent.
Scientific results are not generated in a vacuum. Social processes operate throughout, though they are perhaps more evident at the beginning and at the end; that is when the agenda is decided and the results evaluated. It is here in legitimating its activities vis-à-vis Mode 1 knowledge production that the novelty of transdisciplinary activity is most evident and where tensions arise. For example, while it is true that transdisciplinary research is, in its mode of organisation, more fluid and flexible, it also seems to be more transient. It is perhaps for this reason that in large projects, such as the mapping of the human genome, the constituent expertise remains distributed throughout. There seems little pressure to centralise such large projects on a permanent basis and continuous training of young researchers, technicians and postdoctoral fellows takes place through mobility in existing networks. This mode of training stands in sharp contrast with the monopoly held by the university departments which award the PhD as a prerequisite for entry into Mode 2 work settings.

While knowledge production within traditional disciplinary structures remains valid, interesting and important, Mode 2 is growing out of these structures and now exists alongside them. Although they are at an early stage of development, some of the practices associated with the new mode are already creating pressures for radical change in the traditional institutions of science, particularly the universities and national research councils. Not surprisingly, some of these institutions are resistant particularly to those changes which seem to be threatening the very structures and processes which have been created to protect the integrity of the scientific enterprise.

Quality Control
To some extent, the identification of this change hinges on what is meant by science and technology. What counts as knowledge is, in both cases, to a large extent determined by what scientists and technologists say shall count, and this involves, implicitly if not explicitly the norms governing the ways they produce knowledge. Not only do those claiming to produce scientific knowledge have to follow certain general methods, but they also must be trained in the appropriate procedures and techniques. To be funded, researchers must formulate the problems on which they want to work in specific ways recognisable to their colleagues, and they must be scrupulous in reporting their results to a community of their peers using prescribed modes of communication. Science is a highly structured set of activities involving a close interaction between technical and social norms. Of course, not all science is produced in exactly the same way, but technical and social norms are accommodated differently in each

specialism which in turn, becomes absorbed into the larger community by a process of professionalisation and institutionalisation. Technology is a similar form of knowledge governed intellectually by structures which guide research and suggest likely solutions, and socially by groups of peers who evaluate solutions and develop codes of best practice.

By contrast, what is produced outside of these structures can be problematical. Many argue that knowledge cannot qualify as scientific if it is produced outside its legitimating structures. A tension with established structures will arise when any scientist acts in a manner different from that prescribed by their specific set of technical and social norms. But as long as the numbers of such deviants are not significant, no threat is presented to the social control of knowledge production. However, when significant numbers of scientists choose to work on problems that lie outside their specialisms, when they form teams with other specialists to work on complex projects, when in doing so they enter into arrangements with other social institutions which broaden the constituency of interests involved in setting agendas and priorities, and when performance is evaluated by an expanded peer group, then the legitimacy of outputs may be called into question. In most industrialised societies, the higher education system has seen to it that sound research procedures have been diffused and the number of opportunities to use science has been expanded. The norms that have governed the production of scientific knowledge need to be adapted because the current ones are no longer perceived to be adequate for the continuing development of science itself.

In discussing knowledge production in terms of the emergence of Mode 1 alongside Mode 2, we have to clarify where the differences lie. Of these, an essential one concerns changes in the mechanisms which assess the quality of knowledge produced. In Mode 1 for both scientific and technological knowledge this is a matter of establishing a provisional consensus among a community of practitioners. The judgements of this community form a powerful selection mechanism of problems, methods, people and results. It is a crucial social process to maintain standards and its prerogatives are protected because rigorous control of quality is seen to be the principal way to maintain autonomy over the internal affairs of the community. Quality control has two main components; one is institutional and concerns the spatial position of a particular research activity in the cognitive landscape; the other is cognitive and pertains to the social organisation in which such research is performed.

The dependence of quality control on institutional space   In Mode 1, control is exercised by different types of knowledge producing institutions each of which has its own boundaries, structures of apprenticeship and rules of behaviour. Such institutions include, for example, universities, national academies and the professional societies. Each has different ways of controlling membership, some provide training, establishing procedures whereby knowledge is produced and validated. Because knowledge production in Mode 2 occurs within transient contexts of application it is unlikely that the communities of practitioners who exercise quality control will be backed up by relatively stable institutions such as one finds in Mode 1. Looked at from the point of view of Mode 1 such a process of quality control necessarily appears as dislocated. It takes on transient and temporary forms, exhibits fluid contours and provisional norms, and occupies temporary institutional spaces which can accommodate knowledge producers with many different institutional affiliations, either simultaneously or sequentially.

The dependence of quality control on the social organisation of research
The second component of quality control relates to mechanisms that define what problems are to be pursued, how they are to be tackled and which results shall count as valid. This involves a shift from control located within disciplines to more diffuse kinds of control that reflect the transdisciplinary nature of the problems being addressed. In Mode 2, success is defined differently from that in Mode 1. Success in Mode 1 might perhaps be summarily described as excellence defined by disciplinary peers. In Mode 2 success would have to include the additional criteria such as efficiency or usefulness, defined in terms of the contribution the work has made to the overall solution of transdisciplinary problems. In both cases success reflects a perception of quality as judged by a particular community of practitioners. But, all quality control is linked, legitimated and, ultimately, receives its credibility and scientific authority from an idea, image, or concept of what constitutes good science including best practice. For example, at different times in history what constitutes good science has been guided by the ideal of truth and the search for unitary principles. In Mode 2, the issue of assessing the quality of good research is twofold. One has to do with the fact that the community of practitioners is transient and transdisciplinary, as we have already shown, the other arising out of the fact that the criteria of quality are not solely those that obtain in Mode 1 but include the additional criteria that arise out of context of application.

Currently conventional wisdom is that discovery must precede application. Although this has not always been the case it has provided a powerful image of how things ought to be. By contrast, Mode 2 quality control is additionally guided by a good deal of practical, societal, policy-related concerns, so that whatever knowledge is actually produced, the environment already structured by application or use will have to be taken into account. When knowledge is actually produced in the context of application, it is not applied science, because discovery and applications cannot be separated, the relevant science being produced in the very course of providing solutions to problems defined in the context of application. Those who exert quality control in Mode 2 have learned to use multiple criteria not only in general, but in relation to the specific results produced by the particular configuration of researchers involved.

The Dynamics of Mode 2 Knowledge Production

In order to understand better the growth and diffusion of Mode 2 a distinction will be drawn between homogeneous and heterogeneous growth. Within the scientific enterprise an example of homogeneous growth would be the expansion of a given entity, say papers in nuclear physics, where the rate of growth often follows a logarithmic curve. In this case, growth essentially consists of the production of more of the same, whether these are numbers of papers produced or numbers of scientists working in a given field. The result is exponential growth which would continue indefinitely were it not for the fact that resources are finite (De Solla Price, 1963). Heterogeneous growth, by contrast, refers to a process of differentiation through which rearrangements of component elements take place within a given process or set of activities. In these cases it is the number of rearrangements that grow rather than solely the number of outputs, that is, a shift in the pace of internal differentiation occurs. Considering only national research and development (R&D) statistics in the aggregate, or listening exclusively to the rhetoric of the institutional leaders of the scientific community, may mask the phenomenon, but it is evident that deep-seated structural changes are taking place in the relationships both within and between the scientific communities and society at large, with knowledge becoming socially distributed to ever wider segments of society. The globalisation of science and R&D sourcing and the role that specialised knowledge has come to play in technological innovation result in a highly differentiated, heterogeneous form of growth of knowledge. This is expressed tellingly in authorship patterns of scientific papers, the traditional vehicle of scientific communications. Not only is the average number of authors per paper increasing, but much more significantly, so are the diversity of specialisms and disciplines involved in the writing of a single paper and the range of institutions and organisations from which the authors originate. In addition, the geographical distribution of these institutions continues to broaden. In Mode 2, not only are more actors involved in the genesis of knowledge but they remain socially distributed.

What kind of model, or analytical framework, might best describe this process of heterogeneous growth, a process of diffusion in which the numbers of linkages between entities increases and new configurations are set up, which dissolve and re-emerge in different combinations? Communication plays a central role in this process and the density of communication appears to be the key variable. An increase in the density of communication is an indication that the rate of diffusion is increasing, and given a multitude of different sites of knowledge production and sufficient diversity among participants, growth is likely to be heterogeneous rather than homogeneous.

During the past decades most industrial countries have been putting in place the basic infrastructure for a dynamic knowledge production system based upon specialisation and disciplinary structures. This has involved building up many more universities and research centres of various kinds, often through government research contracts and procurement, encouraging corporations to become significant performers of R&D. Investments in this pattern have established not only a flourishing research culture but also have vastly multiplied the number of sites at which scientific research could be conducted, not only within particular nations but world-wide. In an unplanned and unforeseen way these past investments have established the essential preconditions for the numbers of communication linkages to become large enough to change existing patterns of knowledge production in a fundamental way. The density of communication between the elements of the global research system has reached the criticality which makes a significant expansion of communication linkages a certain, though unintended outcome. The expansion of the number, nature and range of communicative interactions between the different sites of knowledge production leads not only to more knowledge being produced but also to more knowledge of different kinds; not only to sharing of resources, but to their continuous configuration. Each new configuration becomes itself a potential source of new knowledge production which in turn is transformed into the site of further possible configurations. The multiplication of the numbers and kinds of configurations are at the core of the diffusion process resulting from increasing density of communication. Its precondition is the vast increase in the numbers of communicative interactions of many kinds, because only a fraction of these will result in new configurations, which are sufficiently stable to become sites for further knowledge production. This process has been greatly aided by information technologies which not only speed up the rate of communication, but also create more new linkages.

The expansion of the numbers of communicative interactions which underlies the notion of the density of communication includes communications which take place within a particular specialism as well as those which take place between specialisms. Functionally, as well as in its historical evolution, the increase in density rests upon an interrelated three-tiered system, where each level depends upon the other two. In the production of scientific knowledge communication occurs between science and society at large, among scientific practitioners and also with entities of the physical or social world.

Communication between science and society   This is the widest, and by the very nature of the communication link, the most loosely linked web of communication. Traditionally, communication between science and society was essentially one-way: scientists were the holders of privileged expert knowledge, while the lay public was to be enlightened and educated. In the past various forms of popularisation of scientific knowledge have shaped this relationship, without altering the basic underlying conception. The pressure for increased accountability arises in two distinct but related ways. First, in all countries there is now much greater pressure to justify public expenditures on science. Financial accountability is essentially about justifying expenditure, about ensuring that financial resources have been spent in the manner stipulated in the allocation process. But, second, this is only one aspect of a much broader social concern with the conduct and goals of scientific research. There has been an increased demand for social as well as financial accountability.

Enhanced social accountability, particularly evident in the last few decades, arose as a better educated citizenry placed new demands on science. These demands were nurtured against the background of a number of techno-political controversies. In the public debates around these controversies it became obvious that a strong requirement for social assessment of science and technology had taken root in society. The previous one-way communication process from scientific experts to the lay public perceived to be scientifically illiterate and in need of education by experts has been supplanted by politically backed demands for accountability of science and technology and new public discussions in which experts have to communicate a more 'vernacular' science than ever before. The most sensitive domains so far have centred upon technological risks, notably those connected with nuclear power and other hazardous large technical facilities, environmental concerns covering a wide range of topics from the ozone layer to biodiversity, and potential dangers or ethical issues associated with biotechnology and genetic engineering. In all these cases, technology has perhaps been more implicated than science per se, while in the mind of the public the two are seen as closely intertwined. What is at issue very often is the claim that research knows no limits – with the counterargument asserting that not everything research can learn or do, should actually be learned or done, nor is it always beneficial to society. A related argument is that it is no longer possible to contain scientific and technical experiments in the laboratories properly speaking and that society itself has become a laboratory for experiments that ought to be controlled in a more societal and tighter way.

The new demands for accountability and for more communication between the community of scientific and technical experts and the 'attentive' public are interconnected and emanate from the spread of higher education through society. The increased level of education of the population in highly industrialised societies, and the widespread use of technological applications in households, workplaces and in other public (for example, transport) and private (for example, health) places all accelerated the wide diffusion of scientific and technological knowledge into society. As many detailed studies of market-oriented technological innovation have shown, the presence of potential buyers and users directly in the contexts of development influence the direction that innovative lines of research will take (Von Hippel, 1976, 1988).

New forms of knowledge production can, as they diffuse, make for ambiguous situations as older demarcation lines and boundaries become more porous or break down altogether. For example, universities can adopt 'values' from the corporate culture of industry, bringing forth an entirely new type of academic entrepreneur. Conversely, big firms adopt some of the norms of academic culture, for example when they give employees sabbaticals or provide other forms of training possibilities. On a broader level, intellectual 'property rights' have become a major issue on the campus, thereby giving new roles to the lawyers rather than committees in resolving conflicts and in regulating the conditions under which research is performed. The list of examples can be extended almost indefinitely. Through what mechanisms do such 'borrowing' or transfers of norms and practices occur, and how does each subsystem maintain its distinct identity and founding values according to which it resolves other conflicts?

The mixing of norms and values in different segments of society is part of a diffusion process which at the same time fosters further communication among them by creating a common culture and language. In addition, a variety of inter-systemic agencies or intermediary bodies establish themselves in the interstices between established institutions or their components; examples from the United States might be the Occupational and Safety and Health Administration, or the Friends of the Earth, a governmental agency and a private organisation respectively, both concerned with environmental quality, both crossing disciplinary lines and both involving public, private and scientific interests, people, resources and powers. Thus while different kinds of institutions are able to maintain their own distinctive character and functions, they continually generate new forms of communication to link them together. This partially explains the emergence of new hybrid communities, consisting of people who have been socialised in different subsystems, disciplines or working environments, but who subsequently learn different styles of thought, modes of behaviour, knowledge and social competence that originally they did not possess. Hybridisation reflects the need of different communities to speak in more than one language in order to communicate at the boundaries and in the spaces between systems and subsystems. The availability and willingness of large numbers of people to become members of such hybrid communities, however, is also due to the spilling over of scientific attitudes,(which we have loosely defined as a greater readiness to ask questions, and to seek answers through reason, and evidence and the acceptance of change in general), from universities and laboratories to society at large.

Thus, communication between research and society increasingly takes the form of diffusion processes that carry scientific and technological knowledge into society while social norms and expectations held by different institutions and communities are brought home more forcefully to the research communities. At the same time, the sites in which knowledge is created proliferate, increasing both the possibilities and the need for such diffusion. Communication becomes more dense in line with the evolution of overall societal complexity.

Communication among scientific practitioners   Scientific communication linking the sites of knowledge production is carried through the flows of scientists and scientific ideas among them. The density of communication among scientists is embedded in the social organisation of their work. It was realised at the beginning of modern science that a division of scientific labour would be a crucial factor in speeding up the solution of scientific problems. Already in the sixteenth century, Kepler had remarked upon the division of labour among the astronomers of his time: if they were more numerous they would not only be able to gather more observational data, but also by applying their scientific work to a few highly selected problems, they could contribute more efficiently to solution of the problems.

Communication among scientists is influenced by two factors: one is their mobility, while the second relates to how they set priorities and select problems. Mobility, is an essential precondition for the cross-fertilisation of scientific ideas and know-how. Scientists moving between different sites of knowledge production exchange ideas and know-how, and learn about new techniques, devices and principles. Numerous instances of scientific creativity, of sudden insights and the opening up of novel pathways towards solutions can be traced to encounters between scientists brought together from different sites. The more mobility a science system permits or even encourages, the more potential instances of this kind can be expected.

Of course there are limits to mobility as well, imposed by the necessary balance between stimulating fresh insights and the laborious process of working them out. But it is obvious that the density of communication among scientists through various forms of mobility has been greatly increased in recent decades. Numerous conferences and meetings are complemented by a wide assortment of different communication channels, ranging from the old-fashioned article to pre-prints, from phone to fax to electronic mail and multiple networks that allow many minds to meet and discuss issues together without being physically present in the same place. And it is not irrelevant that the world-wide network of electronic mail is heavily subsidised by governments, making its use essentially free to its users.

The multiplication of both formal and informal communication channels has meant a stupendous growth in the density of communication. As recent examples, from the initial news about the discovery of high temperature superconductivity or the alleged success in achieving cold fusion show, the scientific community displays all the features of a global village. Almost instantaneous communication offers scientists working even in remote places the possibility of duplicating experiments immediately, drawing in new experts and exploiting novel ideas. The sheer range of possibilities for new forms and intensities of communication also opens up, at least in principle, the growth of communication between different specialisms, an important aspect of Mode 2 knowledge production. While in the past scientists were more limited in the means of communication at their disposal and used them mainly to communicate within their own specialities, modern information and communication technologies provide them with a widened spectrum of opportunities.

Transdisciplinarity has been facilitated through the availability of these enhanced means of communication. The computer itself has become the new and powerful tool in science which generates a new language and images. One can cite the beautiful coloured images of fractals that have changed the perception of scientists and the general public in ways that are both aesthetically pleasing and mathematically challenging. Modelling data, whether related to environmental research where huge climate or ocean flow models are being generated, or within geography and related disciplines where the advent of geographical information systems (GIS) have literally changed the way of seeing and practising regional planning, have opened new channels of communication cutting right across scientific disciplines and fields of research. Through the inclusion of images and other modes of representing data, an entirely artificial world of representation continues to be created, attesting to the powerful creativity of these new forms of scientific communication. All aspects of Mode 2, and especially transdisciplinarity are increasingly strengthened through these new modes of representation that cut across disciplines while greatly adding to the density of communication with nature and among scientists.

The second factor affecting the increased density of communication among scientists and their research sites arises out of the ways they select problems and set priorities. It is obvious that not all problems deemed worthy of investigation will actually be studied by a critical mass of scientists large enough to make a difference. Characteristic differences in the ratio of people to problems exist between disciplines and specialities.

This allows Becher to compare the 'urban mode' of communication, which he sees as characteristic of the hard sciences with a 'rural mode' which is characteristic of the soft sciences (Becher, 1989: 79–80). As in an urban area, the cognitive territory in the former case is densely packed and crowded by people who all want to work on a small number of problems which are thought to be highly relevant and rewarding. The cognitive space is therefore crowded, communications thick and competition intense. By contrast, many, though not all of the soft sciences and practically all of the applied sciences seem to be marked by a 'rural' form of communication. Problems considered worth working on are much more numerous and widespread; scientists have a lot of choice, and can settle in the next valley if they think the current one is already overcrowded. Communication patterns are less well organised, and news about significant conceptual or methodological advances trickle down rather than spreading rapidly. Hence scientists working in an urban mode must have established mechanisms that allow them to agree more easily on the problems. It is then possible to delineate a more or less common frontier of knowledge and to speak about the kinds of problems that everyone would expect to be relatively near solution, with others perceived to be still further away in the future. A 'rural' mode, by contrast, would also entail a slower pace of collective scientific advance, more dispersed intellectual resources and also with individualistic ways of working. Density of communication between scientists is therefore an important factor in accelerating knowledge production, not just across a variety of different sites, but also on a single, heavily populated site, where problem space is scarce and the price of cognitive territory correspondingly high.

Another important factor in the patterns of communication between scientists relates to the international and local or national dimension. The way that impinges upon competition and cooperation among scientists and the kinds of issues that arise for research organisations still largely embedded in national systems, will be described in a later chapter. Here, it will suffice to re-emphasise that communication among scientists is both essentially international, in line with the universalism of science, and locally or nationally-oriented, in line with the still dominant national orientation of R&D funding. The career structures of scientists, their international mobility notwithstanding, are still largely shaped by the national science system; hence the perpetuation to some degree of different national styles or national traditions of knowledge production.

Communication with the entities of the physical and social world
Communication in this sense is a metaphorical way of describing how scientists approach the object of their study. Ever since the beginnings of modern science in the seventeenth century, ideas about how to 'make nature speak', how to 'induce her to reveal her secrets', or even ways to

'force her to answer' have been used as a way of describing, the experimental set-up and the preconditions framing it. From Galileo's time onwards, the main and most successful language to be used in communicating with nature has been a formalised discourse using mathematics and other kinds of formalised symbols. However, the scientific-conceptual side of this dialogue has always been matched by a forceful communicative practice of attempts at manipulation and control. The practical side of experiments entails craft-work, skills, knowledge and, of course, instruments and technology.

What, then, has changed between the beginnings of modern science and the hi-tech forms of communication with nature that dominate science today? Science has made it possible to observe, analyse and partly to manipulate the 'very large and the infinitesimally small' as exemplified by experiments conducted in space on, say, gravitational waves or the first steps of manipulating individual atoms on the microscopic level of matter. In any laboratory, nature is not just present, but has to be brought in. Then and there, nature is thus appropriately prepared, and can be deliberately subjected to experiments. Through proper preparation it has become possible to speed up or slow down processes, to enlarge or miniaturise according to experimental design. In doing so, instrumentation has been the indispensable working tool, while being far more than merely a piece of technology. Scientific instruments embody scientific knowledge while leading to the generation of further scientific knowledge. They are looked upon, correctly, as a major source of scientific innovation, while often providing important core elements to engender also further technological innovation, once they are transferred from the laboratory to other sites of knowledge production. In short, on the level of communication with nature there has been a stupendous growth of techniques, sophistication of concepts, instruments and tools that have increased the richness of the language in which scientific communication is carried out. The modes of speaking have matured and increased. The experimental sciences not only use symbols, such as those of mathematics, but an array of new devices and instruments, such as STM, the scanning tunnelling microscope or other experimental practices of an empirical kind to achieve this end.

The field sciences such as parts of biology or geology that cannot rely on experiments, have had to develop other methods to converse with nature, while still relying on carefully compared, dated and assessed empirical evidence of fossil records and of geological strata, mineral deposits, plant life and the like. They, too, seek a form of communication with nature, where nature is ready to tell its history in all its details and local variations. Here, too, new instruments and methods, such as the greatly increased sophistication of dating methods for geological and fossil samples, have opened up new possibilities for asking ever new questions. At present, scientists have begun, for instance, to work systematically on the environmental history of the earth. Paleoclimatology seeks to unravel the major changes in climate conditions the earth has lived through and under what conditions they occurred. In making the earth speak, so to speak, and tell its own history in terms relevant to the understanding of today's environmental stresses, implies a combination of methods and models, of observational data and measuring methods for inference, that taken together provide a new degree of communication density in working towards such goals.

These examples from the experimental sciences and the field sciences show that communication is not a phenomenon limited to the social sciences and the humanities. Social scientists also attempt to make their subjects speak, while historians are well aware that the reinterpretation of history never ends. In the humanities, a philosopher such as Derrida (1976) claims that the text can be made to speak for itself and even against itself. In all these cases, meanings and interpretations are involved. Elements from the past, as in history, or from a text, as in literary criticism, are chosen self-consciously and critically, in view of present theoretical or social relevance and future-related significance. Communication with nature or with society is never an end in itself. It remains linked to the interests and social practices of those who communicate.

All sciences, however, have to develop methods and check their interests to prevent nature or its analogue telling them only what they, the scientists, want to hear. They have to make sure that communication remains authentically communicative; in the sense that not all possible interpretations or answers are acceptable, but only those that have been carefully safeguarded against scientists hearing their own voices in a kind of echo effect. When they practise science, scientists behave as realists. They believe that some kind of reality exists out there, with which they have established a suitable form of communication not only verbally or conceptually, but in a robust, technical sense as well. If we accept that scientific theory and practice are intrinsically underdetermined with regard to a reality supposed to exist out there, we can begin to appreciate how much society must be present to constitute the language that allows the filling of the interstices and gaps in this dialogical form of communication with nature. The more sophisticated and complex society becomes, the more dense will be the content and form of the dialogue with nature. A highly developed and technologically sophisticated science, therefore, can produce ever denser forms of communication.

To continue the metaphor, communication with nature is impregnated with social syntax, semantics and technological pragmatics. It can spread if local sites in which this form of communication can be practised multiply, as it is likely to do when the number of scientific practitioners, that is competent speakers, increases. But any form of communication is not primarily quantitative, but a complex qualitative phenomenon. The richness of any communication does not depend primarily on how many words are used, but which ones and in which context. And since communication is essentially open-ended, it allows not just for one, but for an increasing number of possibilities of expression and representation, depending upon the specific characteristics of each site and context. A well developed language allows one to say (almost) everything; hence, the open-ended nature of scientific advance. But no language, no form of communication, can be uncoupled or disembodied from speakers and from the speech events they create. Language, and any form of communication, remains highly context specific, since semantics, the attribution of meanings, is an inherent feature of communicating. The greater the ability to master a language the more attention has to be paid to the context in which communication occurs. If everything can be said, it also becomes obvious that not everything is, or in fact, will be said. Hence, priorities and selection mechanisms will be established intentionally or unintentionally. If the local sites of communication with nature are multiplied progressively, questions of what is being produced there begin to matter.

Some Congruent Substantial Innovations
The dynamics of Mode 2 knowledge production that we have characterised in terms of the fruitfulness of the contexts of use and application, and by renewed channelling of exchanges and patterns of communication, is not just a matter of form or process. It is also a matter of substance or content, as Mode 2 is practised at the frontiers of some techno-scientific research. The more important among these substantial matters include: the widespread recovery within science of an interest in concrete and particular processes and systems rather than in general, unifying principles; the search for knowledge through design whether in physical or biological systems; the constitutive role of computational models in the intellectual and experimental behaviour of scientists and technologists.

The recovery of interest in specific, ordered structures   There is occurring a profound and widespread shift in the rationale of scientific enquiry. Modern science, in its first phase, was characterised by the search for first principles; for example, the search for an abstract mathematical formulation of the rules governing the motion of matter in space and time. In this, Newtonian physics was triumphant and provided the first, highly successful exemplar of what science ought to be. However, it seems that nature is more subtle than is allowed by models of mathematical physics and, as empirical method diffused, so science has relaxed, but not abandoned, its search for first principles and devoted itself more and more to trying to understand natural phenomena and processes using whatever ideas, techniques and methods would yield that understanding. The use of increasingly sophisticated technical means to explore the world, that is to collect data, and using this to test a wide range of intellectual structures is an example of this trend. This expansion of the technological means has made possible a vastly more sophisticated analysis and has allowed the diffusion of many of these techniques from one discipline to another. This is well illustrated by the history of nuclear magnetic resonance which diffused from physics through chemistry to biology and to its current use in medical diagnosis. This approach to nature has been extremely fruitful of ideas and discoveries as well as of practical applications and does not seem to have been much delayed by the failure to find a set of first principles in nuclear science. On the contrary, it has produced a growing awareness of the power and range of empirical methods which have supported a growing interest in the concrete and the particular. This shift may be seen not only in the gradual replacement currently of physics by biology as the exemplar of science but, more generally, in the abandonment of any ideal to which all sciences ought to aim. Instead, there is a pluralism of approaches which combine data, methods and techniques to meet the requirements of specific contexts.

Knowledge through design   One consequence, related to this general concern with understanding specific, ordered structures, is the intention to use this understanding to predict and control their operation in specific conditions. While the production of knowledge with practical ends in mind has always occupied an important place alongside gaining a better understanding of the physical and social world, continuous innovation through applying scientific and technological knowledge in different contexts has reached a new level. The bio-sciences, materials science and computer and information science, for instance, are now structured with a broad interest in application in mind. The current search for the architecture of fifth generation computers lies behind, or in front of, much of the current research into very large scale integration of electronic switches, and no small amount of the physics of semiconductors or the mathematics of fuzzy logic. While many of the problems in these areas possess an intrinsic intellectual interest for those who work on them, this interest is also continuously nourished by research and practical interests of other users as can be seen in genetics, electronics, mathematics and physics. Rather than pushing science into intellectually sterile backwaters, as was once feared, the expansion into ever new contexts of application provides attractive and challenging environments. A reiterative intellectually fertile exchange of concepts, methods and instrumentation continues to widen our understanding of both natural and artificial phenomena, and with it the possibilities of manipulating and controlling them.

One important aspect of this still early development, is that it has become possible to reverse the conventional procedures for making certain substances such as molecules, chemicals and materials. Instead of purifying natural substances or resorting to complex reactions to obtain those with the desired properties, the required materials can now be built up atom by atom, or molecule by molecule, by design, in order to obtain a product with specified properties and possessing certain desired functions. It therefore has become feasible to design a far greater range of materials than previously; the prospect of sciences completely devoted to fabricating artificial materials in this way has become possible. In this regime the product and the process by which new materials are made become integrated in the design process, including specific uses and functions the product is intended to fulfil. Fabricating processes becomes more efficient not only in terms of costs but more importantly, in terms of reduced adverse environmental impact while opening up an entirely new range of possibilities (as claimed especially by the proponents of 'artificial life').

Computational modelling Since both the design of specific materials and their fabrication are increasingly controlled by computers, this opens the way to developing routines that are independent of particular applications and can be used to meet a wide variety of needs. The design and production of a new generation of advanced materials are therefore critically dependent on information technology. This highlights the importance of information technology (IT) infrastructure and communications in the whole research process and the emergence of a science and technology based upon computations. The experimental process with its underlying trial and error approach in the empirical world, is increasingly complemented, if not in part replaced, by new computational models of simulation and dynamic imaging.

References

Barnes, B. (1985) *About Science*. Oxford: Blackwell.

Becher, T. (1989) *Academic Tribes and Territories*. Society for Research into Higher Education. Milton Keynes: Open University Press.

Derrida, J. (1976) *Of Grammatology*. London and Baltimore: Johns Hopkins University Press.

De Solla Price, D.J. (1963) *Little Science, Big Science*. New York and London: Columbia University Press.

Foray, D. and Conesa, E. (1993) 'The economics and organisation of 'remote' research programes: beyond the frontier of knowledge', *Private Communication*.

Jantsch, E. (1972) *Technological Planning and Social Futures*. London: Cassell.

Von Hippel, E. (1976) 'The dominant role of the user in the scientific instrument innovation process', *Research Policy*, 5 (3): 212—39.

Von Hippel, E. (1988) *The Sources of Innovation*. Oxford: Oxford University Press.

Weinberg, S. (1993) *Dreams of a Final Theory*. London: Hutchinson.

2
The Marketability and Commercialisation of Knowledge

Summary

In Mode 2, knowledge production becomes part of a larger process in which discovery, application and use are closely integrated. One important mechanism by which this happens is the expansion of the market for knowledge and the increased marketability of science (and not only of technology). The driving force behind the accelerated supply and demand of marketable knowledge lies in the intensification of international competition in business and industry. In many cases in-house research is no longer sufficient to meet competitive demands. In order to commercialise knowledge, firms have to look for new types of links with universities, government laboratories as well as with other firms. In this chapter we explore some of the parallels between industry's search for economies of scale and of scope and the production of scientific and technological knowledge by research organisations. In both cases intensified competition is at the centre of the demand for specialist knowledge. The combination of economies not only of scale but of scope with dynamic competition shifts the locus of added value in the innovation process, involving firms more closely in Mode 2 knowledge production.

Economies of scale also apply to knowledge production in the academic and government research system especially where large, sophisticated technological systems and rational techniques of management are involved. But comparatively little investment and concern has gone into distributing the results of research which transcend the communities of specialists that these laboratories serve. This institutional separation of production and distribution has created the very language of knowledge transfer as well as attempts to move research oriented institutions closer to the marketplace and to the public sector. But as long as the norms and rules governing Mode 1 knowledge production prevailed and as long as it was believed that whatever item of technology which entrepreneurs wanted would be available as a stream of inventions, the incentives to encourage the diffusion of research could be ignored. The situation changed because research costs rose more quickly than inflation as a result of the familiar sophistication factor. Research budgets came under chronic strain. The use of research for economic purposes has again moved into a central position in the science and technology policies of many countries, although it is often overlooked that in many advanced sectors of science and technology, knowledge is already created in the context of application.

Next we explore the role that competition plays in the generation of knowledge. We maintain that this role is not widely understood. Firms that wish to compete in the international marketplace are confronted with competition as a dynamic process, meaning that later decisions and investments are constrained by prior ones and therefore can either not be reversed or only at a high cost. Moreover, the criteria of admittance to the competitive game change in novel ways. Collaborative ties come to play an increasing role in the way actors behave. Finally, the rules governing competition evolve according to the enabling capacities of new technologies. The traditional concept of competition rules out the possibility that rivalrous behaviour can have beneficial effects for individual firms. Operating the new dynamically competitive environment means working with regimes of knowledge production similar to Mode 2, which are based on both competition and collaboration and on the ceaseless reconfiguration of resources, knowledge and skills. Firms are required early on to choose particular design configurations as well as associated dominant competences which are embodied in the creativity of its scientific and technological workforce and in the infrastructure of the particular firm. The ultimate success of the firm depends on the potential of this creativity and infrastructure in response to market demand. Collaborative relationships are welcome because firm-specific knowledge accumulation (as well as capital investment) is dependent upon a larger, possibly global, environment in which knowledge is being produced (and capital invested in research).

In the final section of this chapter we take a closer look at changes in the organisation of production and distribution of technologies that have sustained continuous economies of scale by delivering productivity gains in the past. The current productivity crisis raises the question whether the technologies on which mass production rests are approaching their inherent limits and if so, what will replace them. High profitability in businesses is linked to their use of specialised knowledge and their customers' willingness to pay a premium for services or goods which meet their needs. Knowledge-intensive companies remain highly profitable because they possess skills not found elsewhere, including brokering skills which are necessary to link problem solvers and problem identifiers.

The future shape of knowledge production has to be seen in the context of the changing nature of the global economy and of ever new configurations of knowledge. In this, information technology systems clearly play a crucial role. At the same time, the notions of competence become redefined and boundaries of organisations tend to become blurred. Problem solvers, problem identifiers and strategic brokers move back and forth. Knowledge resources are held in different organisations and can be shifted between environments which are at one moment competitive and at another collaborative. This is another aspect of the increased volatility of markets. If competition is not checked by novel arrangements for cooperation, volatility may lead to serious breakdowns. Likewise – as evidenced by public controversies and the growth of hybrid fora in which public demand for social accountability is generated as well as articulated – competition for socially distributed expertise in these hybrid fora both diversifies and expands the market for this kind of knowledge. In such an environment, where both uncertainty and volatility are in the ascendant, planning itself turns into an experiment and is to be seen as part of a longer-term societal experimental learning process.

In the previous chapter, we have introduced the notion of a new mode of knowledge production which we have called 'Mode 2'. In Mode 2, we argue, scientific, technological and industrial knowledge production are becoming more closely connected. Moreover, the growth of these interconnections has the character of a diffusion process, with the rate of diffusion related to the density of communications with nature, with other scientists and with society. As the new mode spreads there is a broadening, or reinterpretation, of the norms and values traditionally associated with disciplinary research. As a result, many areas of the most dynamic sciences, the boundaries between disciplines are dissolving and giving way to a more open structure where varieties of knowledge and competence are combined and recombined in novel configurations.

The idea of a new mode of production is useful in drawing attention to how specialised knowledge is being absorbed into a larger process in which discovery and application are more closely integrated. So far we have considered only the supply side of this development. There has, in addition, been an expansion on the demand side. The market for knowledge – the number of places where it is wanted and can be used – is now wider and more differentiated than it has ever been. This is due, in part, to the growth in the numbers of people who are qualified in some scientific or technical discipline, and have been trained in the methods of empirical research. In general, such individuals seek to solve problems using the frameworks and methods they have been taught and sources of information with which they are already familiar. The increased marketability of science is due to the fact that those who possess specific skills are willing to be brought together, even in temporary multidisciplinary teams, to work on difficult and challenging problems. Indeed, that may be the only condition under which they are able to find work appropriate to their training and skills. Alfred North Whitehead observed many years ago that the brilliance of the nineteenth century was not the discovery of any particular invention but the discovery of the method of invention. In the late twentieth century, both the supply and demand for such discoveries and inventions have expanded and accelerated along with the creation of new conditions and places for making them.

The mutual acceleration of both the supply of and the demand for knowledge is being driven by an intensification of international competition in business and industry. The sources of this competition derive in part, from the growing numbers of players on the international scene who have developed their industrial capabilities to the point where they can challenge the traditional manufacturing elites, the UK, USA, Germany and, increasingly Japan, in a wide variety of markets, particularly those for mass produced goods. This pressure has provoked the segmentation of traditional markets and accelerated the search for the relatively safe haven of a niche market. But as the capabilities of the newcomers have increased, niche markets have begun to disappear, and some economists are warning that the only safe haven is pre-eminence in technological innovation (Thurow, 1992). The growth of business enterprise funding of R&D during the period 1980–1988 is given in Box 2.1. For this, in-house research is no longer sufficient; specialist knowledge has to be drawn from a wider range of sources.

Box 2.1
Industrial financing for R&D

Most of the industrial financing for R&D goes to sustain in-house scientific work. But there has been a marked increase in extramural funding for research, especially in Public Sector Research System (PSRS). Again, this varies considerably by country, by sector and even within sectors. On average, only about 4 per cent of total PSRS activity is funded by industry – with the US figure approaching 8 per cent, while as a proportion of industrial R&D expenditure this represents, again on average, about 1 per cent. Some countries, such as Germany, Sweden and Norway, exhibit twice this level of funding.

It would appear to be the case that in general, industry's contribution to PSRS is marginal despite the heady predictions in the press and policy literature during the 1970s. Nevertheless the table below shows a steady increase in real terms in the amount that industry is financing in PSRS.

Business enterprise finance in public sector research system, 1985 prices, $m

	1980	1981	1982	1983	1984	1985	1986	1987	1988
Australia		7			9		14		
France		26	27	27	33	42	45	82	
Germany		52		147		159	176	201	170
Italy	9	25	23	5	8	20	16	16	26
Japan	64	67	78	88	117	125	137	158	
UK		51		57		77	126	119	
US	305	344	372	413	486	561	698	763	816

Source: Webster and Ektowitz (1991), p. 21.

A crucial problem facing the advanced industrial nations bears precisely on this last point. Firms differ in their ability to commercialise knowledge, while competitive advantage lies with those that are successful in doing so. For too long, commercialisation has been understood largely in terms of the application and exploitation of existing knowledge. In the new competitive regime, commercial success requires the ability to generate knowledge using resources which are not stored in-house but distributed throughout a vast, and increasingly global, network. To be able to commercialise knowledge nowadays means that often firms have to play a part in its production. They have to develop new types of links with universities, government laboratories and other firms. Commercialisation is more complex than envisaged in the traditional linear model, where science leads to technology and technology satisfies market needs. Technology is not a commodity, available 'off the shelf'; nor can it be guaranteed through technology transfer or intellectual property agreements alone. More often, it needs to be developed to meet the circumstances of a specific firm.

Scale and Scope in Knowledge Production

A distinction between economies of *scale* and economies of *scope* is crucial to understanding the dynamics of contemporary knowledge production. Economies of scale are the gains made possible by the combination of technology and organisation in which the number of units of production or distribution increases while unit costs fall. Economies of scale characterise a particular form of technology and market interaction that has been successfully exploited for many years and contributed extensively to sustained corporate growth. Industry's search for economies of scale has had a parallel in the production of scientific and technological knowledge. Big science and big technology have often been regarded as being organised on an industrialised pattern. The analogy is far from exact, but in scientific as in industrial production there are efficiencies to be gained by skilfully blending a range of technological and specialist skills under a management regime. Economies of scope, in contrast, are gains arising from repeatedly configuring the same technologies and skills in different ways to satisfy market demand. Firms seeking economies of scope need continuing access to knowledge of many different kinds and, to acquire the necessary access, they are increasingly drawn into its production.

Increasing marketability, the growing demand for knowledge and the spread of Mode 2 knowledge are linked through dynamic competition. Intensifying competition still provides the imperative for innovation but increasingly this involves the generation of new knowledge. To meet their requirements, firms need to participate in this process and are entering into new collaborative arrangements which have many of the characteristics of Mode 2 knowledge production. These linkages highlight the role of new knowledge configurations in the innovation process; and these configurations cross not only disciplinary but also institutional boundaries. Inexorably, dynamic competition is shifting the locus of added value in the innovation process towards a firm's competence in configuring knowledge resources. Such competition between firms, best described as a search for economies of scope, involves them more closely in Mode 2 knowledge production. Their involvement is continuous and forms the basis of their future industrial competitiveness. This does not mean that economies of scale are no longer a source of competitiveness. Just as with Mode 1 and Mode 2, so the need for economics of scale and scope interact. However, increasingly economies of scale depend upon obtaining economies of scope which embody knowledge produced in Mode 2 in different parts of the production chain.

Distribution of the Results of Research
In the recent past, firms often sought to control more and more aspects of their environments. Continuous profit growth and predictability depended upon being able to innovate using technologies which would yield economies of scale over a considerable period of time. This phenomenon has been analysed recently by the business historian Alfred Chandler (1990). It is primarily manufacturing enterprises, he argues, which have been responsible for economic growth in the developed economies of the world. They have provided the fundamental force for change. But, as Chandler has observed, what is often overlooked in accounts of the origins of advanced industrial economies is that firms which have successfully generated economies of scale have done so by employing a three-pronged investment strategy; in production, management, and distribution. In particular, he points out that it would not have been possible to secure the benefits from the large investments in technology and the management of production unless these had been supported by parallel investments in distribution to ensure that outputs were actually sold. Although distribution was, at the beginning, primarily concerned with selling standard products, it gradually became a crucial conduit for conveying information about changing customer preferences. The development of distribution, in turn, constrained the straightforward pursuit of economies of scale by forcing firms to broaden the range of products they could produce with broadly the same production technology. Contact with customers, then, provided an incentive to explore the possibilities latent in economies of scope.

In knowledge production, similar forces are at work. The industrialisation of science can be described in terms of the adoption of economies of scale, and of industrial management practices. Organisations such as CERN or the Brookhaven Laboratories, or, indeed, the University of California with its 150,000 employees spread across nine campuses and three national laboratories, are large, managed, research enterprises which can be compared, in terms of people employed, with many large corporations. To some extent the expansion of their research outputs can be attributed to the application of economies of scale originally worked out in industry. However, the analogy cannot be pushed too far because research managers do not aim to expand their operations in order systematically to drive down their costs to achieve some optimum cost per publication. Laboratories are not usually in competition with one another in this respect, though that may be changing (Martin and Irvine, 1984).

While many university and government laboratories operate with large and sophisticated technological systems which demand large investments and rational management techniques, so far, and with some important exceptions, little investment has gone into the distribution of the results of research much beyond the community of specialists that these laboratories have been set up to serve. As Chandler indicates, in business terms, such behaviour would have been disastrous for firms while mounting stocks of finished goods found no markets.

However, as long as universities and government research establishments were relatively isolated from markets, there was little incentive for them to seek outlets for the results of their research beyond their research communities. Only recently, largely because of slowing growth, have these institutions been forced to consider who their customers are and whether or not the knowledge generated and the services performed can be sold to generate independent revenue streams. In the UK, the Rothschild Report (1971), despite its radical interpretation of the role of government-funded research, limited itself to encouraging research establishments to find customers in the productive sector while academic science was exempted from direct involvement in the achievement of national objectives. At the same time, however, in Sweden the new emphasis on sectoral research was designed to encourage universities to work more closely with the public sector. Other countries also tried to move their research oriented-institutions closer to the marketplace.

The lack of interest and investment in distributing research results has led to many of the institutions of science and, to a lesser extent technology, becoming isolated in universities and government research establishments respectively. Indeed, this institutional separation created the language of technology transfer because initially the task was seen as moving knowledge across institutional boundaries. Although links between science, technology and industry remained friendly the flow of ideas, theories and experimental findings from universities and government laboratories to industry has been uneven. Historically, the classic examples of strong links between the academy and the productive sector include chemistry in Germany and the agricultural research universities, and the land-grant colleges in the USA during the nineteenth century.

More recently, in the USA and the EU's R&D Framework programmes, there have been renewed attempts to build strong links between the academy and the productive sector. Examples in the USA include the research supported by the National Institutes of Health (NIH), the large military projects centred around MIT, Berkeley and Stanford and their adaptation to the civilian economy, or the science parks as well as networks and centres of excellence being built up in various parts of Europe. What is remarkable here, is not so much the intensified interaction between universities and industry but attempts by both to adapt to a novel situation. Today there is less government and more private initiative, more revolving doors than single one-off relationships with specific firms. This generates new problems regarding intellectual property rights and secrecy.

This novel situation has arisen partly because of the rising cost of research associated with the need to incorporate new technologies in the experimental process. Technological sophistication has certainly put research budgets under chronic strain, but a more significant factor than rising costs was faltering economic performance, reflected in falling productivity growth during the 1980s. This has reopened the question of the role played by government funding of science and technology (S&T), and stimulated the search for radical solutions to the problem of tying knowledge production to wealth creation. After a decade of reliance on market forces the science and technology policies of many countries are placing greater emphasis on the public funding of research for economic purposes. Increasingly, both industry and government see the problem less as a need to generate more knowledge than of making use of what is already available; less in terms of supporting basic science than in terms of application of knowledge to wealth creation. Sometimes this has been seen in terms of distributing knowledge which already exists thus bringing it to bear on industry's problems. For example, politicians frequently refer to the massive amounts of information collected by government-funded programmes for satellite observation of the planet. They claim that only a fraction of this has been analysed and turned to any practical or commercial use. More should be done to use existing data before resources are allocated to developing highly sophisticated systems to collect new data. Paraphrasing Chandler's analysis, they argue that appropriate investment in knowledge production and its management has been made. The need now is to strengthen the distribution network by increasing the flow of knowledge from universities and government research establishments to the centres of wealth creation.

But much more is involved. The problem is not so much with the application of existing knowledge to industrial uses but that at the forefront of many of the advanced sectors of science and technology, knowledge is now generated in the context of application. Its mode of production is what we have described as Mode 2 and in this mode the knowledge produced is already shaped by the needs and interests of some, at least, of the potential users. In Mode 2, because production and distribution of knowledge are much more closely related than they were in Mode 1 which still provides so many of the models and metaphors for technology transfer, it has become more difficult to stand outside the process of knowledge production and hope to explain its results later. In brief, both industry and academia must become participants in the production of knowledge which has wealth creating potential. This amounts to a new social contract for the institutions that have funded scientific research.

Intensified international competition is forcing governments to reconsider the function of their S&T investments and firms to become more active participants in the production of knowledge. In doing so both are effectively extending the range and influence of Mode 2. In the next section, the constitutive role that knowledge plays in the competitive process will be discussed. Competition is essentially a process of discovery. Increasingly this involves the generation of knowledge which satisfies user needs.

Dynamic Competition and Knowledge Production

The role that competition plays in the generation of knowledge is not widely understood. The dominant doctrines of economic theory have developed a notion of competition which does not recognise that the nature of competition changes according to historical circumstances. Today, competition is experienced as a force in a process of continuous change, a process in which knowledge is generated not only about the market itself, but also about the physical world and technologies which shape it. Later decisions and investments are constrained by prior ones, and to reverse them is either not possible or carries high economic and social costs. These are the key elements of dynamic competition.

In industry competition implies rivalry, and rivalry means behaving differently from other firms in a way which conveys competitive advantage and alters the prevailing balance between rival producers. However, the traditional concept of competition seems to rule out the possibility that rivalrous behaviour can have beneficial effects for individual firms. Actions taken by firms to enhance their competitiveness such as price reductions, improvement in product quality and advertising campaigns are seen as imperfections which diminish competition, introduce elements of monopoly and reduce efficiency. This paradox, that competitive behaviour is judged to have anti-competitive effects, is at the root of the difficulty of trying to make sense of competition. The simple point is that the competitive process cannot be understood in terms of equilibrium, but only in terms of a process of change driven by differential behaviour. It is because firms strive to be different that a situation can be described as competitive.

Competition is often compared to a race. Any race has three elements: the competitors and their behaviours, a set of rules which determine legitimate behaviour, and the criteria which define success and failure. But in dynamic competition all three elements evolve in a largely unpredictable manner. The criteria of admittance may change to include newcomers, such as universities and government laboratories. The behaviour of actors depends increasingly on collaborative ties and the sets of rules are changed through the enabling capacities of new technologies. Thus, while the criteria which define success and failure do not change in principle, the means through which success is achieved are changed through the role played by knowledge acquisition.

As in any race, there is an ordering of participants. It is the same in economic competition. The possibility of competition depends upon a divergence of views across competitive institutions as to the appropriate strategies with respect to products, prices and modes of production. The mechanisms through which opportunities to behave differently arise and the ways in which competing institutions react to them, are not only central to the competition but also to the strategies adopted to influence the outcomes.

But how does differential behaviour operate? In a dynamically competitive environment businesspeople are working with regimes of knowledge production very similar to those we have described as Mode 2. They need to generate knowledge of various kinds to remain competitive or, to put the matter the other way round, the competitive situation compels them to try to exploit their knowledge bases in particular directions, prompted by what their competitors are doing and by their perceptions of changes in user needs. Usually a firm has to choose a particular design configuration and an associated dominant competence to develop it early on in the innovation process. The firm's future success depends on the wisdom of that fundamental choice and on the ability of its dominant competence to exploit its potential in response to market demands. Just as nature poses questions for science, the market is continually putting questions to the firm. Innovations are the answers. These responses are worked out in an exploratory fashion in which the firm applies its competences to the articulation of its knowledge base. As we have indicated in the previous chapter, this knowledge base is connected in many different ways to the communities of scientific and technological practitioners who provide a distributed resource upon which an increasing number of different people and communities can draw.

For the firm, there is a great deal more involved here than is usually implied under the term 'rational allocation of resources'. Not only is a firm's technology generated in the economic process but the rate and direction of its development is established early on in the innovation process by the choice of a design configuration. As a result, the dominant competence of a workforce and infrastructure of a firm, a subunit or a line of production, are specialised from the beginning and its knowledge base is highly structured and specific. The ability of each unit to enter a new market or to respond to signals from existing ones is always constrained, though not wholly determined by, initial choices and by the creativity of the workforce. In dynamic competition technological innovation is a matter both of resources and resourcefulness.

Box 2.2
The economics of knowledge
production

What makes the market superior is precisely that it organises economic activity around *information*.

Increasingly, there is less and less return on the traditional resources: land, labour and (money) capital. The main producers of wealth have become information and knowledge.

How knowledge behaves as an economic resource, we do not yet fully understand; we have not had enough experience to formulate a theory and to test it. We can only say so far that we need such a theory. We need an economic theory that puts knowledge into the centre of the wealth-producing process. Such a theory alone can explain the present economy. It alone can explain economic growth. It alone can explain innovation. It alone can explain how the Japanese economy works and, above all, why it works. It alone can explain why newcomers, especially in hi-tech fields, can, almost overnight, sweep the market and drive out all competitors, no matter how well entrenched they are – as the Japanese did in consumer electronics and in the US automobile market.

So far there are no signs of an Adam Smith or a David Ricardo of knowledge. But, the first studies of the economic behaviour of knowledge have begun to appear.

Those studies make clear that the knowledge-based economy does not behave the same way existing theory assumes an economy to behave. We therefore know that the new economic theory, the theory of a knowledge based economy, will be quite different from any existing economic theory, whether Keynsian or neo-Keynsian, classical or neo-classical.

One of the economists' basic assumptions is that 'perfect competition' is the model for the allocation of resources but also for the distribution of economic rewards. Imperfect competition is common in the 'real world'. But it is assumed to be the result of outside interference with the economy, that is, of monopoly, of patent protection, of government regulation, and so on. But in the knowledge economy, imperfect competition seems to be inherent in the economy itself. Initial advantages gained through early application and exploitation of knowledge (that is, through what has come to be known as the 'learning curve') become permanent and irreversible. What this implies is that neither free trade economics nor protectionism will by themselves work as economic policies. The knowledge economy seems to require both in balance.

Another of the economists' basic assumptions is that an economy is determined by consumption or by investment. In the knowledge economy, neither seems to be in control. There is no shred of evidence that increased *consumption* in the economy leads to greater production of knowledge. But there is also no shred of evidence that greater *investment* in the economy leads to greater production of knowledge. At least the lead times between increased consumption and knowledge production, or between increased investment and knowledge production, seem to be so long as to defy analysis – and surely too long to base either economic theory or economic policy on the correlation, whatever it might be.

Equally incompatible with traditional economic theory is the absence of a common denominator of different kinds of knowledge. Different pieces of land give different yields; but their price is determined by these differences, that is by the quantity of output. When it comes to new knowledge, there are three kinds. There is first the continuing *improvement* of process, product, service; the Japanese, who do it best, call this *Kaizen*. Then there is *exploitation*: the continuous exploitation of existing knowledge to develop new and different products, processes, and services. Finally, there is genuine *innovation*.

These three ways of applying knowledge to produce change in the economy (and in society as well) need to be worked at together and at the same time. They are all equally necessary. But their economic characteristics – their costs as well as their economic impacts – are qualitatively different. So far, at least, it is not possible to *quantify* knowledge. We can, of course, estimate how much it costs to produce and distribute knowledge. But how much is produced – indeed, what we might even mean by 'return on knowledge' – we cannot yet say. Yet we can have no economic theory unless there is a model that expresses economic events in quantitative relationships. Without it, there is no way to make a rational choice – and rational choices are what economics is all about.

> Above all, the *amount* of knowledge, that is, its quantitative aspect, is not nearly as important as the *productivity* of knowledge, that is, its qualitative impact. And this applies to old knowledge and its application, as well as to new knowledge.
>
> *Source*: Drucker (1993)

The accumulation of capital, insofar as it involves the creation of technological knowledge, takes place inside the firm, but the rate of that accumulation is related to the extent to which the firm has access to knowledge generated by others. This in turn, causes firms to seek collaborative relationships of many kinds: to form consortia (for example, Sematech), to join international programmes (such as Eureka) and to try, by dint of their recognised competence to join networks of various kinds. Such is the nature of Mode 2 that, in these associations, they interact with scientists and technologists from a wide range of institutions who are working on similar or related problems. The pattern of accumulation of knowledge may be firm-specific but this should not obscure the fact that knowledge accumulation cannot be separated from the larger, possibly global, environment in which knowledge is being produced. Some of the implications for economic theory surrounding the growth in importance of information and knowledge are outlined in Box 2.2.

Although this discussion of dynamic competition has largely been in terms of the traditional unit of production it is increasingly applicable to formerly non-economic institutions if they enter the game of dynamic competition.

The Commercialisation of Research

The microstructures of the scientific and technological communities have a formative influence on the ways in which a firm can establish a knowledge base. This influence is exerted through training individuals and by providing them with an orientation; that is, with a predisposition to use certain technologies, to formulate problems and to seek solutions in prescribed ways.

If it is to survive, a firm must specialise. A key question is what provides the focus for a firm's knowledge base to permit the creativity necessary to ensure its survival and growth. Essentially, it is the design configuration which embodies specialised competences, the set of principles which define the purpose, the mode of operation, the materials of construction and the methods of manufacture relevant to some artefact or service.

Design configurations enable the production of a range of products and determine their appropriateness for different market segments. Through the articulation of a particular design configuration substantial economies of scale are achieved on the production side as well as a stream of technical improvements on the product side (for example, the Boeing 700 series, the Phillips cassette). Once chosen, a given configuration locks the firm into a set of choices. Although this may be profitable, it can prevent the firm from moving to new design configurations, so running the risk of being overtaken by technologies in which the firm has no competence. Only if a firm is sufficiently strong to impose its design configuration on the market can this be warded off. IBM which originally was locked into other design configurations had to establish an independent team to make personal computers – and in effect, to compete with itself.

Design configurations, as well as products, play a fundamental role because they form the nuclei around which competition is organised. Firms are constantly attempting to set the technological agenda by trying to establish their design configuration as dominant in a market. Whether the design configuration for recording music is the long playing record (LP), the tape cassette, or the compact disc matters more to the industry than the price of these products. The design configurations are mini-paradigms which impose the technological conditions and constraints within which the firm must operate. They are chosen and developed in the light of the firm's dominant competences, including those drawn from various scientific and technological communities.

The firm, however, is not simply a technological laboratory. It must have a commercial vision as well. This is supplied by the strategic agenda which provides an overall framework within which the internal and external possibilities can be connected. Under similar conditions, firms will differ in technological performance because they have different strategic agendas that function by separating desirable from undesirable technological developments.

Today the commercialisation of research is organised less around the translation of discoveries into new products than in searching for design configurations with the potential to be developed in a variety of ways. In trying to establish their design configuration in the market firms engage in rivalrous behaviour. They try continuously to discover ways to interact more effectively with their environment. By extending their design configurations in ways that attune to markets more accurately than their competitors, their performance is sustained over an extended period of time. As markets become segmented and come to demand more technically sophisticated solutions, firms must become more directly involved in knowledge production which implies participation in a broader collaborative effort. While encouraging cost and risk sharing, such collaborative behaviour undermines efforts to capture market segments.

Maintaining a balance between collaboration and competition has become a central challenge.

The New Economics of Production

The organisation of production and distribution around technologies capable of delivering a stream of productivity increases has been guided by a continuous search for economies of scale. The productivity gains upon which rising standards of living depended, required that each worker be supported with more and more technology, usually in the form of high performance machinery or process plant. Extracting commercial benefit from these technologies, meant that the production process had to be broken up into a myriad of relatively simple organisational routines. By adhering to this approach, firms were repeatedly faced by competition through imitation. So the performance of firms was critically dependent on wage costs. Whenever the technologies of mass production could be easily copied, the production process eventually migrated to those firms, regions or nations, where wages were lowest. In some cases, firms tried to meet the apparent inevitability of rising wages by taking their production activities offshore. However, the low-wage economies to which production was moved soon acquired a development momentum of their own. Many former industrial leaders lost control of what they used to make (Dertouzas et al., 1989). As a result of this diffusion process, the production of many standardised products from motor cars to refrigerators can now be carried on in many places around the world. Not only has this led to a further intensified competition but it has raised serious doubts about the future of the mass production paradigm and its ability to sustain rising living standards (Piore and Sobel, 1984). In the past, of course, similar doubts have been raised which proved to be unfounded because mass production technologies generated another leap in productivity through the application of such notions as lean manufacturing and production (Womack et al., 1990). But doubts persist about whether the technologies on which mass production rests are not approaching their inherent limit and whether more radical sources of productivity growth need to be sought to sustain the current standard of living.

A clue to the answer is provided by considering what is happening within the major production sites around the international economy. In most industries the highest earnings are made when specialised knowledge can be brought to bear on problems, the solutions to which suggest a range of new possibilities. The knowledge being referred to, here, is not narrowly concerned with solving the problems that arise within a chosen design configuration. The design configuration evolves and becomes more and more fixed and, hence, susceptible to imitation. As a result, the products which are an expression of the design configuration can be copied by firms which have not borne the cost of its development but can operate it at lower wages. When imitation is a threat, innovation is a strategy to expand the potential of a given configuration in novel directions that depend on the acquisition and use of knowledge and that cannot be easily copied. According to Reich (1991), the search for non-imitable, knowledge-dependent innovations is happening throughout manufacturing industry whether firms are large or small, whether they are young or old, or whether their technologies are mature or at the leading edge. In other words, knowledge is already a key resource in a regime characterised by imitation. Traditional service industries too are experiencing rapid transformations based upon the utilisation of specialised knowledge. Telecommunication services are transformed by the use of information processing, linking smart buildings and employees in different locations through specialised communication networks. Transportation services, such as road, rail, air freight and shipping, are integrated world-wide through specialised transportation networks and services. Financial businesses too offer a wide range of interconnected services, such as banking, insurance and investment, specialised to meet their customers' demands.

These knowledge businesses are highly profitable not only because of their capability in configuring knowledge but also because of their customers' willingness to pay a premium for services that meet their needs. Knowledge intensive companies remain highly profitable because they possess skills which are not to be found everywhere. While world-wide competition compresses profits on whatever is uniform, routine and standard, that is, what can be produced anywhere, successful businesses in industrially advanced nations respond by producing more specialised products (and so more profitable) and services which satisfy more exactly the needs of customers. Paradoxically, the diffusion of the technologies of mass production and the increased competition that follows in its wake are among the principal sources of the increased marketability of knowledge.

A further point, as Reich, among others, has observed, is that in the knowledge businesses different sets of skills are required if the specialised knowledge they generate is to be appropriated. Problem solving skills are required, in particular the ability to put things together in unique ways, whether they be molecules, semiconductor chips, new alloys, software codes, movie scripts, pension portfolios or holiday packages. This set of skills is distinct from those possessed by the problem identifier whose function is to help customers understand their needs and how these might be filled by customised products. In addition, brokering skills are needed to link the problem solvers and the problem identifiers, and to assemble the required combination of resources, both human and physical.

The emergence of Mode 2 reflects fundamental changes in both supply and demand. The forms are linked closely to the latter, the growth in demand for specialised knowledge of all kinds. This dual growth leads to the multiplication of the contexts of application in which Mode 2 knowledge production can be carried out. On the supply side, specialist training acquired by conventional means may be necessary but it is no longer sufficient. When knowledge production is carried out in a diversity of contexts of application, new skills in configuring knowledge resources (brokering) as well as in problem identification and solution become crucial. Similarly, in the innovation process firms of all kinds become sources of demand for specialised knowledge because competition puts a premium on non-imitability. According to Say's Law, demand creates its own supply. As a result, particularly in the advanced industrial economies, a cadre of businesses is likely to emerge whose competitive advantage lies precisely in their ability to configure and use knowledge. Since these skills do not arise spontaneously and are going to be in increasing demand these developments pose a challenge to existing systems of higher education which are perhaps better adapted to producing knowledge within Mode 1 than with configuring it in Mode 2.

The new economics of production referred to at the beginning of this section, can be interpreted as a shift from the search for economies of scale to economies of scope within the developed economies of the West. Economies of scope derive from the ability of firms to configure their human resources, and particularly knowledge, in novel ways. This gives them a comparative advantage over those who simply adopt and adapt production processes in low wage economies. The dynamo of economies of scope lies in the ability to configure these resources not just singly but continuously. This requirement generates a less constant expansion of demand for knowledge which, in turn, stimulates the spread of Mode 2, on the supply side.

Configurations of Knowledge

This description of the changing nature of innovation in the global economy has important implications for the future shape of knowledge production. Whereas value used to be added by developing technologies which would allow for economies of scale, now these economies need to be augmented or replaced by economies of scope arising from the application of skill and insight in configuring resources, particularly knowledge resources, in novel ways, and doing so not just singly, but continuously.

For any nation, the aggregate of these resources make up its innovation system. It comprises both traditional scientific and technological knowledge producing institutions and the knowledge base of its industries, the entrepreneurship of its public and private sectors and the values cultivated by its schools and universities. In the new, highly competitive global economy the burden of national performance now depends on the ability to configure these resources in novel ways. National innovation systems will not deliver their promise unless ways are found to manage, improve and extend them through networking and other ventures which are at one time collaborative and at another competitive. Managing the national innovation system is essentially about developing human resources. Its managers therefore will have to be skilled at problem solving, problem identification and strategic brokering.

In this respect, competitive advantage lies only partly with the in-house knowledge bases of individual firms. Because of the need to choose the design configurations early, these knowledge bases tend to be highly structured entities and become more highly structured still as the innovation process follows the lines of commercial success. Economies of scope lie in the further elaboration of this knowledge base by creative use of knowledge resources held partly in-house but partly in other organisations. As a result, strategic managers raid other firms for staff, become involved in networks and strategic alliances and enter into collaborative agreements with universities and private sector consulting firms.

In the innovation process, access to accurate, up-to-date information has always been important. But, in the emerging regime, the process of generation, acquisition and diffusion of information will be more and more mediated by information technology systems. The speed of information transmission has increased. The use of computers, satellite transmission and so on, makes knowledge of new scientific data and discoveries, the state of the environment, the ebbs and flows of stock exchange dealings, and the emergence of social trends and new consumer preferences instantly available. Much of this information is stored in computerised data banks linked together in nests of interlocking networks. Access to these data banks has been widened. Large hierarchical organisations are no longer necessary either to create or utilise them.

Participation in the increasing flow of information means more than having more powerful computers or cheap, easy access to terminals. Competence in innovation is being redefined in terms of the ability to solve problems by selecting relevant data and skills and organising them appropriately. When information is plentiful, perhaps too plentiful, competence does not derive from being able to generate yet more, but from the insight gained by arranging what exists in novel ways. Increasingly, this means connecting series of previously independent data drawn from different databanks. This notion of competence may come to define the meaning of 'imaginative'. If this interpretation is correct, a new cadre of specialists will emerge as the problem solvers and problem identifiers referred to above.

The effect of these developments is to blur the boundaries of organisations; to create ambiguity about the proper territory of what is internal and what is external. The job of senior managers, while retaining earlier responsibilities, has gradually shifted over the past decades from managing internal resources, to managing the boundary. Increasingly it will also be their job to manage the external environment. There is no clearer evidence of this than in the area of knowledge production. Problem solvers, problem identifiers and strategic brokers have constantly to work with knowledge resources held in other organisations – universities, government laboratories, consultancies and other businesses. Although there are many differences, managers in higher education are beginning to operate in a similar mode. They must become active partners in a very complex knowledge producing game. A crucial element in this game, is the ability to move back and forth between environments which are at one moment collaborative and at another competitive (see Chapter 3).

New Dimensions of Quality Control

As we have discussed in Chapter 1, scientific and technological knowledge production systems depend heavily and inherently on quality control. So long as science was a relatively simple, internal market of well-known, although novel products (for example, scientists), quality control could depend on and be exercised primarily by members of the scientific elite itself on a largely informal basis. The process began with the education and selection of students, and was controlled subsequently through recruitment into the scientific community and to its elites by the mechanisms of peer review.

When the market expanded and became dependent on external, usually state, funding this informal peer review process was not replaced but rather supplemented by more bureaucratic forms of quality control exercised through committees, commissions and various other procedures. The claim of scientific excellence was maintained as the primary and overriding criterion for judging the knowledge produced and hence the knowledge producer. This chain therefore became an important mechanism for protecting the autonomy of the science system in the face of demands from the state and/or industry. De facto, a trend towards a more routinised and formalised procedure of both ex-ante and ex-post evaluation was established. But, in practice the difficulty of deciding priorities on the basis of a clear distinction between internal and external criteria remained. It is now generally admitted that the internal criterion of scientific excellence per se is a necessary but not a sufficient selection criterion for establishing research priorities. Other criteria now influence the funding system. These require, both in themselves and in combination with other selection criteria, new procedures for evaluation. Since, in principle at least, these forms of evaluation need to cover many stages from the production of knowledge through its marketability to its actual performance in various markets, not all commercial, strategic points of intervention have to be identified which will allow quality control to be exercised and any required changes introduced.

Technological Complexity and Market Volatility
In a similar way, new procedures are needed to establish quality control in technology, both of the actual products and of the processes which have produced them. The problem is not primarily technical, finding the right kind of methods or establishing the correct procedures. Rather, it is one of learning to handle complexity, developing procedures which leave room for experimental planning and preserving opportunities for feedback in order to allow intervention in time to change the course of events, if that is necessary. This problem is intensified by the complexity of Mode 2 knowledge production. For example, large scale projects with a significant technological or scientific component have to face more or less continuous evaluation. So do firms and governments involved in their management. The number of participants in knowledge production is increasing as is the number of 'centres' addressing a particular problem. Further, the whole process is sensitive to the changes that inevitably occur in social, economic and technical environments. The result is volatility and increased uncertainty.

The time when planning meant operations research-based implementation of a series of linear sequencing steps with in-built options and fault-trees, seems to be over. Increasingly, the conceptualisation, selection and realisation of future options are beset by uncertainties or can only be ascertained experimentally in the course of doing the research. For example in the mass screening of women for breast cancer there is no way to improve the effectiveness of testing procedures without making a beginning. Yet, the beginning may not be very effective or may even be counterproductive. Many more loose couplings are needed to allow for possible errors. A range of feedback mechanisms as well as constant monitoring has to be introduced. The key point is that these kinds of control processes are essentially experimental. The accumulation of uncertain or otherwise contingent knowledge is such that it cannot be taken into account in the initial planning process.

The creation of knowledge when both its production and evaluation are pursued simultaneously offers a good example of transverse marketability. Under these conditions a new kind of knowledge is being produced; once created it is in increasing demand. Although it is possible to identify in a rudimentary way the core of expertise and skills, much of this new knowledge is necessarily highly context dependent, and so more likely to be found only in certain configurations. This new knowledge is marketable. The demand for it is evidence of the increasing volatility of environments which arise both inside Mode 2 knowledge production and outside in other markets – commercial or political. The volatility of markets may take certain characteristic forms – for example, be subject to fads and fashions – but the volatility of environments, generally, is more a result of processes linked to internationalisation and globalisation on the one hand, and the tensions and imbalances inherent in the Mode 2 knowledge production, on the other. For example, competition, if not checked by arrangements which allow for and even encourage cooperation, serves only to increase the volatility of environments and to produce the sort of breakdown threatened in the current argument about Japan's meagre contribution to basic science. If Japan will not play a fuller part in the generation of the world's basic science (that is, more collaboration), some nations may be forced to behave in a more isolationist way (that is, more competition) and, in turn, refuse it access to the results of publicly supported research. When research is increasingly produced globally such disputes only increase the volatility of the environment. The inevitable result is a net decrease in the production of knowledge which, in turn, slows the rate of innovation.

Knowledge Production in Hybrid Fora
Of particular interest is the role played by public controversies in the generation of markets for novel knowledge and expertise. Public controversies create meeting places for discussion. Because many diverse actors are involved these meeting places can be regarded as hybrid fora. Controversies frequently lead to the establishment of enquiries dealing with questions of public policy, regulation and a host of other social and ethical issues. New knowledge is gathered, some of it based on the results of previous scientific and technological developments that have gradually become a cause of social concern. For example, new forms of knowledge such as risk analysis, technology assessment or the growth of various specialisms in environmental science, are responses to public concern about the safety of high rise buildings, the adverse effects of traffic, or the effects of global warming. Through these controversies markets for alternative technologies are developed and foci for new research agendas established (Cambrosio et al., 1992). In these hybrid fora not only is there a demand for more knowledge but also, as we have indicated, a specification of the conditions under which it will be carried out and how it will be evaluated. Mode 2 knowledge production contains, as an intrinsic element, a sufficiently open structure to accommodate these increased demands for social accountability. Knowledge in certain areas, particularly those related to environmental issues and choice among technological options is produced in close association with demands for public participation in international, national or local decision making. Competition for socially distributed expertise in these hybrid fora therefore both diversifies and expands its market.

The role played by controversies and the creation of hybrid fora can also be reinterpreted in the light of the more general increase of uncertainty and volatility of the environment. Whenever the kind of experimental planning processes described above fail to work or achieve societal acceptance, public controversies may erupt. They are thus a response to what has already occurred, but also part of the longer-term learning processes based on social experiment and application.

Scale, Scope and the New Mode of Knowledge Production

It is now possible to present an overview of the knowledge production process. First, both knowledge and the sites of its possible applications are increasing through a process in which a new mode of knowledge production – Mode 2 – is diffusing. Mode 2 knowledge production is characterised by closer interaction between scientific, technological and industrial modes of knowledge production, by the weakening of disciplinary and institutional boundaries, by the emergence of more or less transient clusters of experts, often grouped around large projects of various kinds, and by the broadening of the criteria of quality control and by enhanced social accountability. Secondly, Mode 2 knowledge production is matched on the demand side by the growth of niche markets for specialised knowledge. This knowledge is obtained by creative configuring and reconfiguring of competence to meet sophisticated user needs. While this description may not apply to whole firms, particularly if they are large multi-product firms, it does characterise the research-related activities which take place within them. It also helps to explain the growing intensity of competition. This is the third element. The spread of Mode 2 knowledge production, on the one hand, and of market differentiation, on the other hand, is being driven by the intensification of international competition. This dynamic competition does not merely reallocate existing resources but seeks through experiment to discover configurations of knowledge which convey a commercial advantage, and on a recurrent basis. In this process new knowledge is created which provides the base for the next set of advances. Dynamic competition, itself, is a response on the part of the advanced industrial nations to the economic recovery of many countries since the end of the Second World War; to the diffusion of mass production technologies based on economies of scale to an increasing number of industrialising countries; and to the globalisation of competence in research and development. As a result the locus of value-added production has shifted to those parts of the process which require specialist knowledge not easily replicated. Just as the scientific laboratory was the organisational form that fed ideas and inventions through the filter of economies of scale to the technologies of mass production, so the transient research clusters of Mode 2 will increasingly produce the specialist knowledge that through the economies of scope will come to characterise the knowledge industries of the future.

References

Cambrosio, A., Limoges, C. and Hoffman, E. (1992) 'Expertise as a network: a case study of the controversies over the environmental release of genetically engineered organisms', in N. Stehr and R.V. Ericson (eds), *The Culture and Power of Knowledge: Inquiries into Contemporary Societies*. New York and Berlin: Walter de Gruyter.

Chandler, A.D. jr, (1990) *Scale and Scope: The Dynamics of Industrial Capitalism*. Cambridge, MA: Harvard University Press.

Dertouzas, M.L., Lester, R.K. and Solow, R.M. (1989) *Made in America: Regaining the Productive Edge*. Cambridge, MA: MIT Press.

Drucker, P.F. (1993) *Post Capitalist Society*. Oxford: Butterworth-Heinemann.

Martin, B.R. and Irvine, J. (1984) 'CERN: past performance and future prospects I – CERN's position in world high-energy physics', *Research Policy*, 13: 183–210.

Piore, M.J. and Sobel, C.F. (1984) *The Second Industrial Divide: Possibilities for Prosperity*. New York: Basic Books.

Reich, R. (1991) *The Work of Nations: Preparing Ourselves for 21st Century Capitalism*. London: Simon and Schuster.

The Rothschild Report (1971) *The Organisation and Management of Government Research and Development*. Cmnd. 4814. London: HMSO.

Thurow, L. (1992) *Head to Head*. New York: William Morrow.

Webster, A. and Ektowitz, H. (1991) *Academic-Industry Relations: A Second Academic Revolution?* London: Science Policy Support Group.

Womack, J.P., Jones, D.T. and Roos, D. (1990) *The Machine that Changed the World*. New York: Maxwell Macmillan International.

3
Massification of Research and Education

Summary

All industrialised countries have experienced a rapid growth in the development of mass higher education following the Second World War. In this chapter we explore some of the most salient characteristics that the participation in formal secondary and higher education has taken and some of the consequences for the higher education systems. Other changes can be seen in the character and aspirations of the student body, in the curriculum, in modes of governance, in relations between students and teachers, in forms of finance and in the relations of the universities with other institutions in society. Moreover, the expansion of mass higher education has begun to affect many other institutions of society helping to lay the groundwork for further diffusion especially of technical and scientific knowledge and skills throughout society. Mass higher education also created a growing market for new cultural products, as well as underpinning the widespread distribution of initiative and innovation in the economy. Another effect has been the creation of a market for continuing education and an increase in the capacity of the labour force to respond to rapid technological change.

The growth of mass patterns in research both resembles and differs from those in education. The greater part of research is still considered an elite activity, even if carried out by large numbers of people and requires intense socialisation in an academic discipline. But new patterns of research in Mode 2 that emerge in and alongside the universities are related to the process of massification of higher education and are an outgrowth of it. They involve close working relationships between people located in different institutions, and typically include business people, patent lawyers, production engineers and others located outside the university. Research in Mode 2 also requires different patterns of funding from traditional discipline-based research. In the wake of these developments a host of new institutional arrangements emerges, linking government, industry, universities and private consultancy groups in different ways. To a noticeable extent traditional university-based research is threatened by the encroachment of industry and the profit-making mentality.

In the core section of this chapter we identify ten shifts which have accompanied the massification of higher education. They begin with a diversification of functions of the university which may range from the most specialised research to the most utilitarian kind of training. As a result the distinction between the institution's core and the periphery has become less clear. What has also changed dramatically is the social profile of the student populations. In the human and social sciences this change has had a sometimes powerful influence in re-shaping the intellectual content of curricula. Higher education systems have also tended to be no longer dominated by the arts and the sciences, subjects that have been overlaid by education for the professions and professional training. At the same time, however, institutions of higher education have tilted in their basic orientation towards research, thus increasing further the already existing tensions between teaching and research. But alongside the growing prominence of research, an equally important shift has taken place. Emphasis has moved away from free enquiry to problem solving and, more generally, in the direction of problem-oriented research. There is also a widespread decline from primary production of data and ideas to reconfigurations of data and inputs to yield new results. Another shift concerns the broadening of accountability. University teachers no longer enjoy high status and universities form part of a larger and denser network of knowledge institutions that extend into industry, government and the media. An open question concerns the future role of technology in teaching, that is, to what extent teaching will be conducted also at long distance through computers, videos and television. Last, but not least, we see a decisive shift towards multiple sources of funding for higher education, the consequences of which can go into several different directions. The last of the ten shifts relates to the organisational development of the modern university. Faculties, for instance, have become largely administrative rather than intellectual centres, whereas the real academic unit has become the course or research team. Specialisation has led universities to abandon most moral and cultural claims transcending the accumulation of intellectual and professional expertise. We explore the consequences of these shifts for mass access to higher education.

The new institutional arrangements of institutions of higher learning and the new locations of knowledge production in what has become known as the extended university have led to the adoption of more effective managerial models. In them, unlike the old universities, strategic planning is not inhibited by collegial government, nor tough choices obfuscated by the need to secure consensus. They also promise greater flexibility of response. This partial repudiation of collegiality has moved the university closer to a corporate model of management. In turn, private corporations have adopted some principles of collegiality. Yet, the ongoing managerial revolution inside the university is part of a paradox. Just when the university has become a more efficient centripetal institution, the knowledge produced by it has become more incoherent and centrifugal. Disintegration and reorganisation of knowledge production inside the university can take several, also contradictory, forms which are further explored by us.

Higher education thus continues in its transformation, driven by changes in knowledge production and dissemination patterns. The massification of higher education also provides the base from which knowledge industries – in contrast with knowledge-based industries – could emerge. For knowledge industries the knowledge itself is the commodity traded. The system of higher education provides a continuous flow of trained personnel for industry, raising the general level of familiarity with science and technology throughout society. The result is a multiplication of the number of sites where research is a recognisable, professional activity. This process, however, carries its own instability. Many graduates continue to develop specialised skills outside the universities and are now in a position to understand what university researchers are doing. In the future universities will comprise only a part of the knowledge producing sector and they are no longer in a strong enough position to determine what shall count as excellent.

With the intensification of international economic competition, concerns grow over whether enough economic benefit is extracted from university research, which is often seen as a matter of technology transfer. By now, transfer mechanisms

multiply, liaison programmes between the universities and industry develop rapidly, industrial sponsorship of research grows and universities become increasingly involved in regional development. In Mode 2 knowledge production the nature of technology transfer also changes, with the older view of a linear transfer being replaced by a more interactive notion. If technology interchange moves from the periphery of the university to its centre, it is likely to generate a number of significant changes, which we briefly explore towards the end of this chapter.

The development of mass higher education in modern industrial societies after the Second World War exhibited a rapid growth of enrolments, both in absolute numbers and in the proportion of the traditional age grade. This was preceded or accompanied by a very large increase in the numbers of young people, first from middle and then from lower middle and working class origins, who were enabled or encouraged to stay on in secondary school beyond school leaving age to the age of transfer. Almost everywhere this required a reform of secondary education, and the creation of a comprehensive secondary school in place of or alongside the traditional elite secondary schools. A growing fraction of this new population was then enabled or motivated to qualify for entry to some form of higher education, either through passing the entry examinations (for example, A level exams in the UK), or gaining the requisite school leaving certificate (for example, the baccalaureat, in France).

Behind this great increase in participation in formal secondary and higher education were a number of more or less independent forces: the democratisation of politics and society that followed the Second World War; the growth of the public sector that required more white collar workers and university graduates; a growing industrial economy that employed more highly skilled and educated workers; the widespread belief that further economic development depended on educated manpower, especially scientists and engineers; and finally the attractiveness of education itself as a major element of the new welfare states, sustaining and legitimating democratic societies.

The growth in the number of students seeking a university-type education had a number of consequences for the systems of higher education. First, came growth in the old, elite universities; next the creation of new universities; then the expansion of non-university forms of post-secondary education offering different or no degrees, and finally, the assimilation of the new sectors to the degree granting system, and the inclusion in both old and new universities of new faculties and departments representing subjects formerly excluded from them, preparing students for new or semi-professions.

All this involved changes in the character and aspirations of the student body, in the curriculum, in modes of governance, in relations between students and teachers, in forms of finance and in the relations of the universities with other institutions in society. During this period, all forms of higher education admitted more first generation students from lower social strata, many of them mature students, staying on longer, preparing for other than the civil service or the old professions, often married and with outside jobs, and with fewer expectations that a degree gave them the right to secure careers. After some resistance, the curriculum began to reflect the changed nature of the student body, and their cultural and occupational interests. Meanwhile, older elite forms of higher education survived alongside the newer mass forms, in elite subjects, medicine, law, classical languages, in advanced seminars and in postgraduate studies.

The new institutions of mass higher education have begun to affect all the other institutions of society, both by creating large populations of scientists and engineers who spread out through the economy and take over jobs formerly held by technicians, and by producing even larger numbers of non-technical graduates who transform jobs formerly held by non-graduates. Mass higher education also created a growing market for new cultural products of all kinds, and a voting population prepared to support the further expansion of higher education and those aspects of the welfare state employing its graduates and serving their interests. The higher education system also underpinned the widespread distribution of initiative and innovation in the economy, and in several countries, but particularly in the United States, it made possible the explosive growth of small service and high technology industries.

Among the most significant effects of mass higher education, of a special significance for the production of distribution of knowledge, is the great increase in the market for continuing education, and thus of the emergence of a learning society, one in which life-long study, as well as training and retraining, are possible and taken for granted by large fractions of the population. This readiness to learn greatly increases the capacity of a labour force to respond to rapid technological change and is at least as important as the innovations that support it, or the competitive markets that drive it. In this respect at least, the lesson of history has been grasped; a labour force of craftsmen organised around traditional habits and skills is the enemy of technological change, as continuing education is its friend.

Education and training in advanced industrial societies have the paradoxical task of preparing people to perform difficult jobs competently, while bringing them to accept that they will have to change their jobs and skills quickly and often. This requires not only the training in the skills and habits themselves, but the inculcation of positive social attitudes towards change. We can see both clearly in sections of the population which do not possess them – for example, workers in traditional heavy industries, or miners, who have prided themselves on skills in a valued, life-long working class occupation. Those workers, many of them now among the long-term unemployed, have been the real victims of rapid social change, as have been their occupational communities. Modern mass higher education teaches people not to become too closely devoted to one occupation or a single set of skills. It prepares them for the likelihood that both will change often and that they must travel fast. To travel fast one must travel light, in skills as well as attitudes. The only skill that does not become obsolete is the skill of learning new skills. This dynamic of higher education weakens many social ties and institutional links, which if unchanged would hinder social, occupational and geographical mobility. But these changes have also weakened family ties with as yet undisclosed consequences for the character structure of the second generation of postindustrial men and women.

The growth of mass patterns in research both resembles and differs from those in education. For one thing, research is inherently an elite activity, even when carried on by large numbers of people. It is done for the most part by people who themselves have had an elite higher education, at least in their postgraduate studies. In the past, recognition of competence to carry out research arose out of an intense socialisation to an academic discipline. The greater part of research still has this character. But new patterns of research in Mode 2, emerging in and alongside universities, are related to the massification of higher education, and are an outgrowth of it. These new forms of research involve close working relationships between people located in different institutions, not all of whom need be researchers. There are, thus, frequent interactions of university based research scientists with businesspeople, venture capitalists, patent lawyers, production engineers, as well as research engineers and scientists located outside the university.

The research itself is more likely to be part of a national programme directed to some socio-technical goal that may have originally arisen out of a line of academic research. Accordingly, it is likely to be sensitive to its commercial possibilities, and may be initiated or carried forward out of a sense of these possibilities. It may not be reported in the traditional way through scientific conferences and journals, but be confined to reports closely held by commercial sponsors; it may involve shared use of academic and industrial facilities and technology; is more likely to be transdisciplinary, and to be carried on by people whose disciplinary and institutional loyalties are ambivalent.

This style of research has visible consequences for the larger society, and raises ethical and political problems which in turn call for people with special training or sensitivity to those issues both in the generation of research programmes and in their evaluation. As a consequence, social scientists are increasingly being brought directly into research teams. Research in Mode 2 requires different patterns of funding from traditional discipline-based research. It depends less on funding from central government or non-profit foundations, and more on the firms, industries and social lobbies directly involved, though central government may add its money to that of the universities and private industry if it wishes to further research in specified areas.

The conduct of research in the context of application as well as its distributed nature mean that contemporary science cannot remain easily within the confines of university departments or academic centres. This is leading to the emergence of a host of new institutional arrangements, linking government, industry, universities and private consultancy groups in different ways. The tradition of university-based research is threatened by the encroachment of industry and the profit-making mentality and values. On the other hand, researchers in countries with traditions of non-university research feel the need to link their research institutions more closely with universities to be more open to innovation and intellectual competition. The movement of research from the university to other forms of organisation in which the university is only one participant has a parallel in training. A multi-billion dollar knowledge industry has developed outside established educational institutions, responding in more direct, and usually more effective ways to the needs of industry and the labour market. This is leading to the erosion of the monopoly the universities have enjoyed in providing training and granting educational credentials with good currency in the private sector.

Patterns of Massification in Higher Education

A profound transformation of knowledge production inside and outside of universities is currently underway, one which both depends on and contributes to the progressive massification of higher education. In this section we will identify major elements of that transformation with a view to highlighting how they are likely to affect knowledge production not only in the sciences and technology but also in the social sciences and the humanities. Ten shifts have accompanied the massification of higher education as it has taken place in most industrialised countries.

Ten Shifts

Diversification of functions   Across most higher education systems mainstream undergraduate education and postgraduate training have become comparatively less important, as other activities such as part-time study and the continuing education of mature professionals become more important. Universities increasingly serve a growing variety of functions from the most abstract research to the most utilitarian training force. As a result the distinction between an institution's core and its periphery has become less clear. Some traditional functions and activities, like student associations and their cultural activities, are now more periphery than core. The total mission of higher education has become fuzzier and more diverse, more difficult to define and defend.

Social profile of student populations　Students are no longer predominantly male and drawn from the upper middle and professional classes; nor are they destined to fill elite positions in society and the economy. Instead they are drawn from a much broader social base; the balance between the sexes is more equal; and most graduates now go, not to positions of leadership, but to join the vast middle-range salariat of the public services and private corporations. As higher education becomes a more common experience, prospective students are less often drawn away from their families and homes. Instead they often stay in place, enriching the lives of their own communities rather than refreshing metropolitan elites. The more equal balance between women and men, combined with the growth of feminism, has been a powerful influence reshaping the intellectual contours of many subjects, especially in the human and social sciences. This is a good example of how higher education's changing social profile has radical effects on what its members think it worthwhile to study and teach. Also the democratisation of graduate origins and destinations means that the core skills and liberal values of higher education are being reinterpreted in different ways by groups which bring into the university the cultural and political currents and conflicts of the larger society. As knowledge production moves out of the university into the larger society, so the society's diverse values move in. The boundaries of the university are increasingly blurred by both tendencies.

Education for the professions　Modern higher education systems are no longer dominated by the arts and the sciences. These core subjects have been overlaid by layers of professional education – first, the liberal professions; then by technical professions, principally the many branches of engineering, and the technical sciences that accompanied the successive waves of industrialisation including the latest wave of the information sciences; the caring professions which were stimulated by the growth of the welfare state; and most recently the new upsurge by the enterprise professions, centred upon business, management and accountancy. The next wave may well have the environmental sciences at its core. The intellectual effects of the shift from liberal education to professional training have been often observed but their cumulative effect may only become decisive now in reshaping higher education.

Tensions between teaching and research   Paradoxically, although higher education has moved towards a mass system of teaching large numbers of students, its fundamental orientation has tilted towards research. The product of elite institutions is seen to be knowledge in the form of scientific publications and technological devices rather than in the form of trained young minds. Most teachers, even in non-elite institutions, have reshaped their professional ambitions accordingly. The acceleration of knowledge production in the research enterprise serves to highlight the provisional character of all knowledge. It becomes increasingly difficult to sustain a coherent undergraduate curriculum weakening even further the traditional concern of the universities to provide trained minds.

Growth of problem-oriented research   Alongside the growing prominence of research an equally important shift has taken place in its character. Less and less it is curiosity-driven and funded out of general budgets which higher education is free to spend as it likes; more and more it is in the form of specific programmes funded by external agencies for defined purposes. This shift is also reflected in a changing view of university research. The emphasis has moved away from free enquiry to problem solving – perhaps with too little regard being paid to problem definition and articulation. It is also reflected in a changing economy of research; projects are constrained by specifications of increasingly expensive equipment and by specialised skills of researchers. It is hard to obtain support for research which is not cost conscious, leading to a rationing of equipment and personnel. The result is a squeeze of both actual and intellectual research possibilities entailing their concentration in certain locations only.

Decline of primary knowledge production   The emphasis in many research fields has switched from primary production of data and ideas to their configuration in novel patterns and dissemination to different contexts. One reason is that primary research has become very expensive because it requires access to sophisticated equipment and highly expert staff. In the social sciences and humanities there has been a drift away from monographs, which are more costly, to works of synthesis which are cheaper to produce. Another reason is that advanced information technologies have made research results quickly accessible and ubiquitous. Active researchers no longer need to cluster, physically, around sites of primary knowledge production. Finally, the reconfiguration of new knowledge can be as exciting a process intellectually as is primary production.

Broadening of accountability   Another shift in higher education is from being inner-directed to becoming outer-directed, not in the sense of David

Rieseman's celebrated characterisation of postwar America but in reference to the self-image of universities as autonomous institutions. They perceived themselves largely as self-contained and self-referential institutions. Practices such as peer review and academic tenure still reflect this view. University teachers once enjoyed high social status. Today, higher education appears in a different light. Universities form part of a larger and denser network of knowledge institutions that extends into industry, government and the media. Both their autonomy and their monopoly position are reduced. This is reflected in a diminished social status of higher education teachers and in their relationships with other professional groups and the market. Knowledge is generated across rather than in self-sufficient institutions.

Technology for teaching   Formerly students were taught in classrooms and laboratories, face-to-face and, ideally, in small groups. In the future it is likely that they will be also taught through computers, videos, television and at a distance. One result might be that undergraduate education will be transformed – for the better, if new technology encourages independent learning; for the worse, if it creates an alienating anti-humane environment or leads to mechanistic forms of learning. Another result might be to weaken further the already weak links between teaching and research. Teaching and research may occur in different places and be funded from separate sources. Intellectually they may grow apart because technology-assisted teaching needs to be highly structured while research will deal increasingly with indeterminate knowledge.

Multiple sources of funding for higher education   Although in most highly industrialised countries, the state will remain the predominant source of funding for higher education block-grant funding is likely to be replaced by a more targeted approach, especially in research, and in undergraduate education by allocation mechanisms mimicking the market. At the same time non-state income is likely to become more significant with the state itself encouraging this shift. These changes in funding patterns will result in important intellectual consequences reinforcing the separation between research and training. The targeting of research funds is likely to lead to more mission-oriented research. But greater pluralism of research funds will also contribute to intellectual diversity, counter-acting perhaps other prevailing trends.

Efficiency and the bureaucratic ethos   The last of the ten shifts in higher education is the least tangible but perhaps the most important one. It has two aspects. The first is the easily understood process of specialisation and fragmentation that has accompanied the division and sub-division of knowledge up to now. This cognitive phenomenon has marked the organisational development of the modern university. Faculties have become organisational rather than intellectual categories; even departments are seen as largely administrative units rather than as intellectual centres. The real academic unit has become the course or research team. The second aspect relates to the pressure of remorseless specialisation that has led universities to abandon most moral and cultural claims transcending the accumulation of intellectual and professional expertise.

Consequences for Mass Access

Taken together these ten shifts are likely to stimulate further the demand for access to higher education. They underlie trends routinely experienced by students, university teachers, administrators and researchers alike. The shift away from a standardised population of undergraduates is not new. Going on to higher education is rapidly becoming as automatic as staying on at school after the minimum leaving age. The change in student profile away from middle-class males to a more balanced student population in terms of gender and class is irreversible.

Nor will the shift from the traditional arts and sciences to vocational courses be reversed even if tomorrow's students have more diffuse ambitions or none. Vocational courses may take on some of the general functions previously performed by academic courses. Once students were socialised into the prevailing intellectual culture through the classics, more recently through history or economics. In the future, business studies, perhaps with a green tinge, combining today's twin enthusiasms for enterprise and the environment, may fulfil a similar role.

The shift from teaching to research is likely to be complicated by the move towards greater mass access. The scientification of new subjects, by providing them with respectable research bases, will continue to boost research. The incorporation of new institutions into the extended university may stimulate their research ambitions, in the form of action research linked to teaching and professional practice. The need to concentrate research funds, especially at the high-cost cutting edge will, however, encourage the emergence of mainly teaching institutions.

Both the shift from curiosity-driven to problem-solving priorities in research and the decline of primary knowledge production will be further stimulated by the growth of a mass education system. So will the shift from a self-referential autonomy of universities to a greater emphasis on accountability within a denser network of other knowledge institutions. The special privileges higher education could claim when it was still dominated by traditional universities, will be more difficult to sustain when the educational system includes other private and public institutions and agencies, with more mundane functions.

The changes in the now predominant pattern of undergraduate education, the spread of new teaching technologies especially in the United States and the relative decline of small-group face-to-face teaching, are also likely to be encouraged by mass access, mainly on grounds of cost. The extent to which the new technologies will enter higher education and how they will blend with more traditional forms of teaching is still an open question. The move towards plural funding will also accelerate in a wider-access system. Most governments encourage educational institutions to raise additional private income and governments everywhere had to reinterpret their responsibilities for higher education. These are no longer seen largely in fiduciary terms, as a public-interest obligation to maintain a healthy higher education system for scientific, cultural and civic reasons. Instead governments increasingly regard themselves as the biggest and most powerful customer, buying student places and commissioning useful research. At first sight it looks as though this trend will continue as the system moves towards mass access. But it can also be argued that, as higher education takes on some of the universal characteristics possessed by compulsory school and near-compulsory further education and training, to define it in customer–contractor terms will become more difficult. The pressure then will mount again to satisfy less utilitarian expectations and to regain some of its lost civic quality.

The transition will be a highly complex process. Instead of a single strong flow there will be cross-currents, eddies and even undertows. Massification is not leading straight to a Brave New or Big Bad World; its consequences are ambiguous. To explain these trends solely in socio-economic, political and organisational terms as is generally the case, leads to a failure to recognise their complexity and inherent ambiguity. Rarely are they examined in relation to shifting intellectual values and altered constructions of knowledge. Any analysis of higher education institutions must rest both on a perspective from the inside, meaning the scientific nature of knowledge, and on a perspective from the outside, the pressures exerted and expectations harboured by society.

Collegiality, Managerialism and the Fragmentation of Knowledge

Knowledge can no longer be regarded as discrete and coherent, its production defined by clear rules and governed by settled routines. Instead, it has become a mixture of theory and practice, abstraction and aggregation, ideas and data. The boundaries between the intellectual world and its environment have become blurred as hybrid science combines cognitive and non-cognitive elements in novel and creative ways. Similar changes have taken place in the socio-economic order, partly as a result of the impact of technology. Large and rigid organisations have been overlaid by new means of communication and production that are both more fragile and less formal. The impact of this postindustrialism has mirrored and reinforced the drift towards confusion in the intellectual world. In this, the massification of higher education is a key phenomenon. To understand knowledge it is necessary to understand the institutions in which it is produced. The most important of these institutions remains the university or, more accurately, the extended university. But, the traditional university engaged primarily in the formation of academic and professional elites and in pure research is now only a small part of the spreading higher education and research systems possessed by most advanced countries.

Nor is it always the most important part. Alternative institutions, such as the (former) polytechnics in England, once firmly regarded as second-tier, have grown to rival the universities; the so-called corporate classroom has assumed greater importance as the advanced training needs of knowledge-oriented companies have increased; R&D has flourished in an industrial environment. All, or most, of these arenas of intellectual activity can reasonably be embraced within the extended university. The advantages that these new locations of knowledge production have over traditional universities are two-fold. First, they offer more effective managerial models; in them, unlike the old universities, strategic planning is not inhibited by collegial government, nor tough choices obfuscated by the need to secure consensus. Second, they promise greater flexibility of response to fast-changing intellectual and professional needs; they seem to belong to a forward-looking enterprise culture sceptical of the traditional demarcations, taxonomies, hierarchies that clutter the old academic culture.

Tighter management and greater flexibility highlight two important trends. The first is the effect of the managerial revolution that is taking place throughout higher education; this partial repudiation of collegiality has been most marked in new knowledge institutions on the periphery but spread rapidly to the core of old institutions during the 1980s. As a result the university has moved much closer to an industrial pattern of organisation with senior management teams and strategic plans, line managers and cost centres. Just as universities have moved closer to a corporate model of management, so private corporations have become more collegial; large rigid hierarchies of line managers have tended to be replaced by more loosely coupled networks of team managers, at any rate in more forward-looking industries, particularly those prominent in the creation of an information or knowledge society.

Despite this convergence, the effect on the university has been profound. This managerial revolution has not only established a much tighter organisational framework but created at the centre of the university, in its administration, a managerial energy that competes with as well as complements the academic energy of its constituent departments and research teams. This new energy has combined with the older, slower bureaucratisation of higher education to produce institutions that reflect the growing complexity of the modern university and its importance both in knowledge production and in nation maintenance. Together they have redefined the university in organisational rather than normative terms.

There seems to be a paradox here. Just when the university has become a more powerful centripetal institution, the knowledge which is its chief commodity has become diffuse, opaque, incoherent, centrifugal. This has taken three forms. The first is the ceaseless subdivision of knowledge of greater scientific sophistication. Many of today's most creative subdisciplines have been formed by associating previously unconnected fragments of other disciplines. These new fields of enquiry tend to be volatile and parochial, both qualities which undermine the idea of a broader and coherent intellectual culture. The second is that wider definitions of knowledge have come to be accepted, partly because of the erosion of older ideas of academic respectability and partly because of the impact of new technologies. New disciplines have entered the curriculum of the extended university as taboos have tumbled, while technology has not only created new professions which demand new skills but radically affected what is possible in established disciplines. An overarching discipline like information technology stretches all the way from the most abstract concepts of artificial intelligence, which address fundamental ideas of mind and logic, to routine skills training in the day-to-day use of computers. It has opened the way to a quantification revolution not only in the natural and applied sciences but in the human and social sciences as well. The third form of disintegration is the deliberately decentred diversity and incoherence associated with postmodernism. Postmodernism, has become a kind of sub-intellectual patois. Certainly it has become a formidable publishing industry in its own right.

These three forms are contradictory in their details. For example, the subdivision of science into expert fragments can be taken to represent the triumph of positivism; postmodernism can be taken to mark its death. But all three have had the common effect of making it almost impossible to talk sensibly about the wholeness of knowledge. Science no longer has a single strand, no shared method, no common preoccupations, no values which all its various branches share.

Yet what appears to be a contradiction between institutional coherence and intellectual incoherence, or the competition between managerial and academic values for possession of the university's soul, may conceal a deeper complementarity. The development of much stronger institutional management and the more organised coordination of higher education systems may compensate for the waning coherence of science. As disciplines have become less able to provide a firm framework, institutions have had to be strengthened to provide external scaffolding in place of internal strength. If the centre will no longer hold there is a need for institutions as powerful organisations and their mercenary managers. However this dichotomy may not offer a sufficiently sensitive description. A more accurate account might emphasise the growing interpenetration of academic and managerial practice within higher education. In areas such as continuing education, technology transfer and special access programmes for the disadvantaged there is no easy separation between their intellectual and administrative aspects. These hybrid activities are shaped by both centrifugal forces, which reflect the diversity and incoherence of modern science, and the centripetal character of modern higher education with its greater managerial tautness.

It is not simply that the growing institutional strength of the university has compensated for the disintegration of a common intellectual culture, or of values and rules shared by all branches of science. It is rather that academic values and managerial practice have been combined in unusual and volatile combinations. Old demarcations are breaking down between traditional universities and other higher education institutions because both are embraced within the extended university. There, the sharp distinctions between academic and lay players in knowledge production has weakened because the latter play a key role as brokers or even creators, of science; and between teachers and students, because with increasing numbers of mature students and post-experience courses the latter may have alternative skills and knowledge. As these demarcations crumble, more fundamental ones will be called into question – those between theory and practice, science and technology, and even knowledge and culture. These organisational and intellectual transformations are not separate, or even parallel, but contingent phenomena.

Transition to the Knowledge Industries

The dynamics of these changes point to a continuing transformation of higher education. At the core of this process lies knowledge and its modes of production and dissemination. In particular what is meant by science and how it is produced, disseminated and ultimately absorbed into society is undergoing fundamental changes. Important kinds of knowledge are being produced not so much by scientists, or technologists or industrialists, as by symbolic analysts, people who work with the symbols, concepts, theories, models, data, produced by others in diverse locations and configure them into new combinations.

The distinction between those who create knowledge and the symbolic analysts who configure it underlies that between knowledge based and knowledge industries. Knowledge-based industries attempt to understand and improve the operation of a particular manufacturing process. They are concerned primarily with product and process development. By contrast, for knowledge industries the knowledge itself is the commodity that is traded. It is produced in a variety of places – universities, think-tanks, government laboratories – but once knowledge is created it may be available for re-use in some other combination. In the knowledge industries, value is added by the reiterated use of knowledge; reconfiguring it with other forms of knowledge to solve a problem or to meet a need. Firms in knowledge industries compete with one another in terms of the ingenuity with which they configure knowledge. This resource is the ultimate source of their created comparative advantage.

The massification of higher education provides the base from which knowledge industries could emerge. The diffusion of higher education through society had the effect of supplying the continuous flow of trained manpower for the industrial system. Research had already become a central function of the universities; initially in elite institutions, and gradually in others. This process, at first slowly but later with gathering momentum, not only raised the general level of familiarity with science and technology and the methods and procedures of science but also multiplied enormously the number of sites where research as a recognisable, professional activity could be carried out.

This process harbours an instability. By providing increasing numbers of scientifically literate graduates, the universities are continuously working to their own disadvantage by ensuring that the numbers of able, trained people outside universities rises continuously, relative to the numbers of those within.

Many graduates continue to develop their specialist skills outside the walls of the university and are now in the position not only to understand what university researchers are doing but are able to pass judgement on its quality and significance. In the future the institutions of higher education, the universities, in particular, will comprise only part, perhaps only a small part, of the knowledge producing sector. They are no longer in a strong enough position, either scientifically, economically or politically, to determine what shall count as excellent in teaching or research. Accountability – that is, the social demand for quality, performance and value for money – now involves a complex social process of legitimation. Adjustment to these new pressures is changing the traditional organisation and structure of the university system.

Scientific research has become intrinsic to the notion of a university. Most of university research remains very small science, bringing together a professor and a few graduate students. Together, they constitute a nucleus of research activity, the research group. On the one hand, this arrangement is vulnerable; students graduate and leave if the university cannot offer them a position or continuing grants. Newer, younger students are as yet unproven as co-workers; they are an uncertain resource. To overcome the vulnerability associated with small size and high mobility, research groups become opportunistic in their search for research funding. If no long-term funding can be secured, the gap has to be filled by shorter-term, more problem-oriented contract or consultancy work. Research priorities may need to be adjusted, often and quickly. On the other hand, the research group is highly flexible. It is legitimate, even expected, that professors will work on a broad range of topics depending upon their curiosity, scientific interests, competence and their ability to obtain the necessary funding.

From the perspective of the overall research system the need for external funding encourages professors, and hence universities to be responsive to societal demands. Flexibility also enables research groups to change research fields and to move quickly into new exciting areas. From the perspective of industry, this is a valuable asset and one of the reasons why universities are still seen as the primary site of competence in basic research. Since the training of young researchers is an integral part of the research process, the flow out of universities of young, inquisitive minds, assures industry a continued supply of competencies trained in the latest skills and techniques. Industry, then, has a vested interest in keeping the reservoir full and flowing. So far, it has been able to achieve this at little cost to itself.

With the intensification of international competition, the extraction of economic benefit from university research, and from publicly funded research, more generally, is now a matter of concern. It is seen less in terms of need for new knowledge than in terms of commercialisation of what is already available; less a matter of research than of technology transfer. This transformation is one of the most far-reaching that we have described because it involves drawing the universities into the heart of the commercial process. The universities are no longer the remote source and wellspring of invention and creativity but, are part of the problem solving, problem identification and strategic brokering that characterise the knowledge industries. While small university research teams are vulnerable to the mobility of young researchers, their strength lies in the knowledge networks to which they have access by dint of competence and the flexibility with which they can address new problems. These assets make them attractive to industry, and the potential rewards are so great and so important for the university as an institution that no president, rector or vice-chancellor can afford to leave the matter entirely to the whim of individual professors.

The Changing Nature of Technology Transfer

Research in industry, even if conditions are better than in many university laboratories, is always problematic because it has to keep its objectives in harmony with the company's overall strategy. A commitment to basic research is particularly difficult to sustain. It is constrained by time limits and subject to frequent, rigorous evaluations in the light of shifting company fortunes. As research becomes more expensive, and is subjected to strategic and financial considerations its base tends to narrow. As a consequence, to remain competitive industry increasingly needs access to knowledge generated elsewhere. One avenue is to join with other firms in pre-competitive research. Such collaborations are still infrequent. For many reasons, the universities remain the preferred option. However a number of prerequisites have to be met. Geographical proximity is important; it facilitates information exchanges and informal contacts necessary before any, closer, cooperation can be initiated. Close contacts and trust have to be maintained during the entire period of collaboration. Where this is done on a long-term and systematic basis, collaboration has a greater chance of success. The need for mutual accommodation is particularly clear in technology transfer.

There was at the turn of the 1980s a watershed in the history of technology transfer in the universities in the United States and in Western Europe. Traditionally, the transmission of knowledge from universities to industry had occurred through traditional processes: the hiring of graduates, the publication of results of university research in professional journals, and consulting by university staff. In the late 1970s new transfer mechanisms multiplied: university patent offices were created or reorganised; new approaches to obtain value from intellectual property such as equity ownership were tried; liaison programmes developed markedly; industrial sponsorship of research groups and universities rapidly became increasingly involved in regional development plans.

What is occurring is not only an increase in the volume of activity but a transformation of the practice of technology transfer itself. As in Mode 2 knowledge production the distinction between basic and applied research becomes blurred, the notion of technology transfer has to be reconsidered. It cannot any more be understood as a transmission of knowledge from the university to the receiver easily and usually with almost no follow up. Instead it is no longer like a relay race, in which the baton is passed cleanly and quickly from one runner to the next. Technology transfer looks more like a soccer game in which the university is a member of a team. To score it needs the aid of all its team mates. The ball is passed back and forth constantly among the players who may include businesspeople, venture capitalists, patent attorneys, production engineers, and many others in addition to the university faculty. This is why it has been suggested that technology interchange is a more appropriate phrase than technology transfer.

The older view of a linear process connecting discoveries and inventions to the production process is displaced by a more interactive one. While in the linear view, the university was distanced from the commercial process, and could still preserve its academic values, in technology interchange it must become involved at both individual and institutional levels and adapt to new rules. If technology interchange moves from the periphery to the centre of the university value system, a number of significant changes will have to be made (Matkin, 1990). Research universities will make explicit their commitment to technology interchange and reflect this in organisational structures and resource allocation. They will facilitate the involvement of faculty members in activities associated with the commercialisation of results of their research.

Organised units within the universities, staffed by professionals and dedicated to tasks in technology interchange will continue to be formed and increase their activity. Because it is a matter of interchange the major thrust of these units will be to support and nourish relationships with industry. The seemingly disparate activities of corporate donor relations, corporate research partnerships, corporate/university economic development initiatives, student employment opportunities, continuing education, and technology licensing will come to be viewed as part of a single pattern of interactions with corporations which need to be fostered and maintained over the long term.

Research universities that engage in technology interchange will eventually become financial partners in start-up companies created to exploit the university's intellectual property. This financial involvement will extend beyond passive ownership of equity to some form of active participation in the generation of venture capital. In most cases this involvement will be separated from the university through buffer organisations. The financial contributions of industry to the university will steadily increase. These contributions include gifts, research funding, payments of licensing fees and other direct payments for the use of university property, and membership dues and other special payments for access to the university. In addition, the governments as well as the EU will increasingly recognise and reward universities for their efforts to interact with industry.

Such changes will bring criticisms against the university for not being protective enough of their reputation of objectivity in engaging into efforts aimed at commercialisation. This is why clear and well articulated policy and mission statements will be needed, in which the universities emphasise their role in serving society through technology interchange activities. Under such conditions institutions ought to be able to maintain a collegial atmosphere with the notion that faculties owe their primary allegiance to the university. In the long run policies governing university and faculty interactions with commercial concerns will become more process-oriented and less proscriptive in order to protect university values and to shape university commercial involvement. If they wish to play the technology interchange game research universities will have to travel a long way. The needed institutional experiments and transformations will make them different institutions. However, if they do not develop in that direction they will be passed by other knowledge production organisations.

Reference

Matkin, G.W. (1990) *Technology Transfer and the University*. New York: Macmillan.

4

The Case of the Humanities

Summary

In this chapter we extend our argument to the case of the humanities. Although Mode 2 knowledge production and especially its close association with 'science going to the market' may seem alien to the core values and social practices that prevail in the humanities, a closer analysis reveals a different picture. Although the humanities and the definitions of culture as elaborated and inherited from the nineteenth century are commonly regarded as pre-industrial, we argue that many of the characteristics identified by us and illustrated by referring to developments in science and technology, can also be found in the humanities. While this is an easy argument to sustain in straightforward descriptive terms, we have found it much more difficult to come forth with a plausible and satisfactory interpretation of substantive links between values and practices found in the humanities and in Mode 2 knowledge production.

Similarities and correspondences between recent developments in the humanities and the trends we have identified in earlier chapters are numerous and suggestive. We begin with drawing attention to the expansion of output which is as pronounced a phenomenon in the cultural field as it is in science, technology and industry. Yet, this spectacular growth of cultural production is usually little noticed and certainly not given attention equal to the attention accorded to innovation and growth in scientific and technological areas. The reasons for this relative neglect lie in the – wrong – assumption that the humanities' connection to the creation of wealth is weaker and that cultural production is less costly. We show that a much more differentiated assessment is necessary which reveals, partly at least, the deep involvement of certain forms of cultural production with the image production industry and its economy.

This rapidly expanding industry produces diverse and

heterogeneous knowledge, characteristic of Mode 2. We concede that there exist sometimes confusing cross-currents with multi-site production of culture always having been more of the routine than an exception and with the university's aspiration to dominate cultural production being even more unsustainable than in other fields of knowledge production. On the other hand, commercialisation as part of the process of moving directly into contexts of application is surely a feature of the culture industry (with only certain forms of elite production being exempt). In general the humanities are embroiled in markets in a more diffuse sense, because their intellectual values are shaped by the social context in which they are developed and practised. We maintain that cultural products are the symbolic currency in the market of life-chances, just as new technological products underlie the hard currency in the markets of industry.

As we see it, the contrast between pre-social science and pre-scientific humanities is breaking down. Contradictory pressures of social accountability have also reached the humanities in a specific form, as the controversies around political correctness show. As in other areas of knowledge production, increasing demands for social accountability lead to a shift in quality criteria, which are defined no longer within an academic community, but involve validation from other external and often diffuse sources. Transdisciplinarity, another Mode 2 characteristic, is also endemic in the humanities, while the role of instrumentation seems more peripheral, or at least open to future developments, when assessed by the ways in which computers for instance have altered the traditional artisanal work style of scholars in the humanities. Evidence is mounting, however, that information technology is rapidly making inroads upon the substantive content and modelling capacity in certain fields, such as linguistics and that other more subtle impacts are being felt. It is also the case that not only the economy of the culture industry has been influenced by new technologies, but that individual aesthetic responses and the respective notions of literacy and visual sensibility are reshaped in profound ways.

It is with regard to flexibility, however, which is another characteristic associated with Mode 2 knowledge production, that the humanities seem to be most advanced on this dimension in the sense that they draw their intellectual energy from ceaseless interrogations relinking past and present. It is in this respect that a key dilemma is encountered which is felt more accurately by the humanities than in science and technology. Reflexivity requires rootedness, a context in which one can act. On the other hand, reflexivity seems to demand an institutionalisation of doubt and thrives on a certain dose of uncertainty. There is also a marked pressure of secondary works and production becoming so numerous that primary production is completely overshadowed. An analogy with science and technology can be seen in the relative loss of importance of the primary discovery which becomes just one of many necessary ingredients on the long road from initial discovery to marketable products of innovation.

In the last part of this chapter we emphasise the essential contextualisation of the humanities. They do not only exhibit reflexivity in a more continuous and radical manner than the natural sciences. Their reflexivity is expected to carry meaning for the entire human experience. In this regard they differ markedly from the natural sciences, while the social sciences occupy a middle, and perhaps mediating, ground between them. While the social sciences attempt to keep some kind of distancing from what they observe and interpret, in large parts of the humanities and in cultural production no such aloofness is observed to delineate or express meaning. On the contrary, the distance between creation and contextualisation is minimal, and the construction of meaning is considered the essence of what the humanities do.

While we see a number of intriguing correspondences between the growth of modern culture and the transformations of industrial society in which science and technology appear to have been triumphant, many contributions that the humanities have brought to reflect upon them, remain full of contradictions. In the different and often incoherent responses that they have brought to bear upon the human condition, the social reality of the time is critically mirrored and creatively transformed. It seems that the humanities both stand a bit aside as commentators or performers, while at the same time they are deeply involved in shaping powerful cultural images which in turn influence the entire culture of a society and its stratification systems.

The distance between academic and industrial scientists is far less than that which separates scholars in the humanities from those who work in the mass culture industry. Mistakenly, 'science goes to market' is the shorthand title likely to be pinned to some Mode 2 knowledge production. Its characteristics may seem alien to the intellectual values and social practices bound up in the humanities and, more broadly, to the definitions of culture elaborated in and inherited from the nineteenth century. That culture, and so the humanities which are its intellectual representation, are commonly regarded as pre-industrial, even anti-industrial, in their normative inspiration despite their twentieth-century engagement with, and incorporation within, mass markets.

This is an incomplete and arguably an inaccurate first impression. The characteristics identified in earlier chapters and illustrated in terms of science and technology are perhaps more typical of the traditional humanities than they are of the natural and many social sciences. To the extent that Mode 2 knowledge represents a step beyond an inalterable notion of science, the humanities which have resisted scientification (until recently regarded by many scholars in the humanities as a precondition of intellectual robustness) can now be seen to possess, however serendipitously, many Mode 2 characteristics. This is the argument advanced in this chapter. In straightforward descriptive terms it is an easy argument to sustain, although to interpret the substantive links between the values and practice of the humanities and Mode 2 knowledge patterns is much more difficult.

Mode 2 Knowledge in Science and the Humanities: Similarities and Differences

Certainly there are suggestive correspondences between recent developments in the humanities and the trends identified in earlier chapters – the expansion of output, perhaps amounting to an acceleration; the growing fuzziness of disciplinary boundaries, in the shape of transdisciplinarity, the stretching of inalterable definitions of knowledge and consequent declining authority of experts; the increasingly significant role of commercialisation – or, more broadly, the social contextualisation – of knowledge; heterogeneity of knowledge production, or the permeability of frontiers between the university and scientific systems on the one hand and society and the economy on the other; and the massification of research and higher education.

Growth of Output
The explosion of knowledge in science and technology over the past two decades is visible in the stream of new products and services, and the improvement in quality and decline in price of existing products. Behind these technological miracles stand trained people and support for R&D. Two figures can stand for many. In 1970 the five leading Western

industrial nations – the United States, Japan, West Germany, France and Britain – together expended about $125 billion on research and development (in constant 1987 terms). By 1989, those same countries had doubled that figure to over $250 billion, in constant dollars. In 1970 those same five countries employed about 920,000 scientists and engineers in R&D; in 1989 they employed over 1.8 million, almost doubling the number in two decades. (National Science Foundation (NSF), 1990). UNESCO (1988) estimates that in 1970 a little over 2.6 million scientists were employed world-wide; by 1990 that figure had grown to a bit over 5.2 million – almost exactly a doubling in those two decades, consistent with the rate of growth for the five leading Western industrial powers.

One other set of figures may be of interest here. In the US in 1960 private firms, supplied 42 per cent of all American expenditures for industrial R&D, the rest coming from federal sources. By 1990, 71 per cent of the costs of industrial R&D in America was coming from the industries where the R&D was being done. Or looked at differently, over those three decades federal expenditures for R&D by private firms went up over sixteen fold. In constant 1987 dollars, federal expenditures remained almost constant at about $25 billion over those three decades, while private sources went from about $18 billion to about $65 billion over that time period (NSF, 1990: 18).

Moving beyond the realm of science and technology, UNESCO reports that the total number of book titles published in 1960 was 332,000. By 1970 that figure was 521,000; by 1980, 715,000, and by 1990, 842,000, a growth of about two and a half times over that thirty years (UNESCO, 1992). This is perhaps a better measure of the general expansion of 'intellectual activities' over that time period, which saw a continuing steady growth of higher education enrolments world-wide after the explosive growth of the two postwar decades.

The expansion of output is as pronounced a phenomenon in the humanities and the wider domain of culture as in science, technology and industry. The rate of cultural production is increasing as rapidly as that of scientific publication, inside higher education, through the mass media and in the widely diffused culture – or, better, image production – industry. More professors lead inexorably to more books. Since the end of the eighteenth century more than 25,000 books, essays, articles and other commentaries have been published on Shakespeare's *Hamlet*. Every year 30,000 doctoral theses on modern literature are completed in European and American universities.

In the wider cultural arena explosive growth is just as remarkable a phenomenon. To take one example, in 1945 New York had only a handful of art galleries and not more than a score of artists who regularly exhibited their paintings there. Forty years later the number of art galleries had grown to almost 700 and the number of professional artists to 150,000. Art works were being produced at the staggering rate of 15 million a decade, compared with 200,000 in late nineteenth-century Paris. And this is only the tip of the iceberg. These front-line producers of culture are vastly outnumbered by what Daniel Bell has called the cultural mass – 'not the creators of culture but its transmitters; those working in higher education, publishing, magazines, broadcast media, theatre and museums, who process and influence the reception of serious cultural products' (Bell, 1979). By contrast we argue that the transmitters of popular culture are also among its creators. In the humanities socially distributed knowledge has long been a characteristic.

Commercialisation and Rising Costs

There are two reasons why this rapid growth of cultural production is a less celebrated phenomenon than the parallel explosion of scientific knowledge. First, it is assumed, wrongly, that its connection to wealth creation is much weaker. In societies where basic material needs have been largely satisfied, cultural consumption, and so production, have become increasingly significant forms of economic activity. The cultural services sector is an especially dynamic component of the modern economy. And, in a postindustrial society images of all kinds have a symbolic power that can be directly related to material production as well as to ideological reproduction. These issues will be discussed in greater detail later in this chapter.

Second, cultural production is apparently less costly, certainly in the restricted form of scholarship in the humanities. Literary scholarship does not require expensive equipment and instrumentation; its computing needs remain modest. The logistics of philosophy have not changed radically since the age of Aristotle or, more accurately, since the foundation of the great library of Hellenistic and Roman Alexandria. The cost of scholarship in the humanities has been largely absorbed within the infrastructure of rapidly expanding higher education systems.

Humanities scholarship, therefore, is much more intimately related to the massification of the university than scientific research which, to some degree, can be regarded as a separate phenomenon with its own internal dynamics and external imperatives. The humanities, on the other hand, are doubly embroiled in social applications: first, because history, literature, language and other arts disciplines engage from their various perspectives the human condition, whether individual consciousness or social experience (and so are inherently reflexive, an issue which will be discussed in more detail later); and second, because the resources necessary for scholarship and the professional structures in the humanities are largely by-products of the social transformation created by the expansion of educational opportunities, especially at university level.

Of course, if all cultural production rather than simply scholarship in the humanities is considered, costs rise. Multimillion dollar films can reasonably be compared with some big-science projects. But, although vastly more expensive than scholarship in the humanities, the economy of culture, or the image production industry is distinct from those of leading-edge science and high-technology industry. Certain forms of cultural production, of course, like national theatres and museums and metropolitan orchestras, depend on public subsidy. But this subsidy is generally seen not as investment, whether in the context of economic growth or social welfare, but as old-fashioned patronage. Despite its widespread use of commercial language – strategic plans, business sponsorship, matching grants – in its arts policies the modern state behaves much like the Renaissance prince. Similar non-commercial considerations seem to predominate among the necessarily mixed motives of private and corporate patrons of culture.

As a result elite cultural production, if publicly or corporately subsidised, appears to be foreign to much of the characterisation typical of Mode 2 knowledge. But in any case it makes up only a small part of the culture industry, the bulk of which is unambiguously commercial in its ethos, orientation and organisation. Most cultural production is funded by private consumption, individual choices exercised through mass markets, rather than through public or corporate investment regulated by the long-term plans still typical of most science and technology even in the age of Mode 2 production.

Heterogeneity
As a result, this rapidly expanding industry is diverse, producing heterogeneous Mode 2 knowledge. It has a highbrow component, partly reliant on state patronage as in the cases of national theatres or universities but expressed most dynamically through the burgeoning market for exhibitions, concerts and other performance art and – here the link with the humanities in a narrower sense is explicit – for literary and intellectual journals; a middle-brow component, reflected in the mass teaching of the humanities in schools and universities, the ever-increasing sales of standard classics, serious modern fiction and their musical counterparts, the rise of cultural tourism as part of the heritage industry; and a lowbrow component, the all-pervasive popular culture of the modern world produced by mass literacy and the all-powerful advertising images which shape the postindustrial economy. (The two, popular culture and advertising images, interpenetrate each other in a symbiotic if ironical relationship, forming a new hegemony of style.) An example of the heterogenenous nature of Mode 2 production in the humanities and the arts is described briefly for the case of architecture in Box 4.1.

Box 4.1
Postmodernism and architecture

Postmodernism, the most raucous although not most characteristic expression of Mode 2 thinking in the arts and humanities, was an aesthetic before it became an intellectual movement. Its origins lie in playful conjuring with space and form, the transformation of the built environment, rather than in the delicious obscurity of poststructuralist ideas or the temptations of 'deconstruction' in literature.

Postmodernism arose out of a rejection of the so-called 'international style', the austere unadorned architecture which can be traced back to Adolf Loos in Vienna, Walter Gropius and the Bauhaus, and later Mies van der Rohe in the United States. This style, therefore, sprang out of modernism's assumed heartland – Vienna around the First World War, Weimar Germany and, after the rise of Hitler, their transatlantic Diaspora. And, through these associations, modernist architecture was intimately related to wider intellectual currents now regarded as typically modern – Keynesian economics, Joycean prose, the Freudian psyche. After 1945 it became the house-style of liberal democracy and welfare state capitalism. It still dominates the skyline of most modern cities, its rationalist form-and-function aesthetic inspiring equally the skyscrapers of corporate business and the planned estates of public housing.

Postmodern architects have attempted to soften, even to challenge this 'international style' by reattaching ornament, encouraging eclecticism. They reject the canon of modernism that function must determine form. They have mixed-and-matched different styles recklessly but deliberately. Corinthian columns jostle with Egyptian pillars (neither of structural significance) on the facade of the National Gallery extension in London; a few miles upriver Terry Quinlan's Richmond Riverside parodies and pastiches the terraces of Georgian London; and in New Orleans Charles Moore's Piazza d'Italia with pillars of every order and Pop-Art motifs resembles a theatre set more than an urban space.

The aesthetic (or anti-aesthetic) that inspires such architecture aims to amalgamate the professional and popular, high-art and low-art – but not with any desire to synthesise. Incongruity is embraced by postmodern architects. Some, like Charles Jenks (1991), refer to this as 'double-coding', combining state-of-the-art building technology with vernacular and whimsical ornament to create buildings which communicate in different ways to professional and popular audiences. Others, more extravagantly, eschew all rationalisation of the architectural effects which they strive to produce (or which are produced without striving). Their buildings reflect not the public order of the Fordist corporation, or the welfare state, but the private disorder of high-jinks junk-bond finance, the neo-conservative abrogation of social policy. Like this unruly and amoral world they confuse, disorient, even deceive – but also, perhaps, assist a higher aesthetic purpose by undermining those uncritically inherited conventions that govern our view of space and form.

Buildings as stories, or texts that lack any authoritative meaning – the affinities of postmodern architecture and postmodern thought are clear. In architecture deconstructivism; in literature deconstruction. The pastiche and collage of the architect mirror the fictions, the fragmentation, of the intellectual. Mode 2 as expressed in the humanities and the arts, although not to be equated with postmodernism, shares in some of the same impulses – most notably, the mixing of genres, aesthetic and intellectual, the intermingling of high-art and popular culture, the eclecticism of critical authority, the variability of moral criteria.

This heterogeneity is not simply expressed through hierarchy. Indeed the problematical nature of knowledge in the humanities tends to invalidate the very notion of hierarchy as well as to undermine its practical expression. There are confusing cross-currents. Popular culture is the object of academic study. Teachers of literature are themselves writers. Popularisation through television, radio, newspapers and magazines is set alongside monograph-bound scholarship. Multi-site production of culture has always been routine rather than exceptional, although the focus of extra-academic production has switched from the Victorian gentleman-scholar's study, through the publishing house, to the television studio or advertising agency. The concentration of scientific brain power and technological know-how, so marked a feature of the postwar economy, was only feebly echoed in the humanities. The university's aspiration to dominate cultural production was never sustained even at its self-confident apogee a generation ago. To the extent there has been a globalisation of cultural production, it is a mass-media phenomenon in which humanities scholars based in universities have played only a supporting role.

The Context of Application

Three of the key aspects of Mode 2 knowledge therefore – rapid expansion, heterogeneity and contextualisation – are as characteristic of culture and the humanities as of science, technology and industry. The evidence of acceleration in both the wider domain of cultural production and the narrower territory of scholarship in the humanities is incontrovertible. Commercialisation as part of the process of contextualisation is surely a feature of the culture industry, with the exception of certain forms of elite cultural production. In advertising, where the culture industry makes its most direct intervention in the economy, commercialisation is particularly intense. The humanities are embroiled in markets in a more diffuse and plural sense, because their intellectual values are inevitably shaped by their social context and application. By way of analogy, it could be said that they are the symbolic currency in the market of life-chances in the way new products underpin the hard currency in the markets of industry. Outside the academic system individual lives and social experiences are becoming increasingly dissimilar as family structures shift, occupational patterns are transformed and class loyalties wane to be replaced perhaps by new identifications determined by ethnicity or ideology or, most powerfully, far-reaching individualisation. This social differentiation accelerates, and is accelerated by, cultural diversification.

In terms of other closely related Mode 2 characteristics – the generation of knowledge within a context of application, greater social accountability, and quality control no longer determined by scientific quality alone but including wider criteria – the humanities have always been forerunners. Rather than the humanities being pre-scientific, it is the natural sciences which until very recently have been pre-social. In the humanities and the social sciences ideas and social practice have always been intimately related. Successive revolutions, and counter-revolutions in economic thought, the destruction of old mercantilist and physiocrat orthodoxies by Adam Smith and David Ricardo and, a century and a half later, the Keynesian revolution which undermined the authority of classical economics, flowed from the radical changes in the socio-economic environment which had exposed these earlier intellectual structures as inadequate. To take another example, the emergence of literature as a field of academic study was closely related to the growth of the reading public in the nineteenth century; subsequent shifts, and especially extensions, of that public have accounted for the frequent turbulence in literary, cultural and critical studies.

The appearance of cumulative knowledge production in the natural sciences, at any rate during the periods of normal science, to adopt a Kuhnian terminology, and the absence of counter-revolutions, except during the transition from one paradigm to another, therefore can as plausibly be seen as evidence of epistemological underdevelopment as of maturity. It has even been argued that control of the natural sciences has never been wrested for any length of time from the hands of restricted interest groups – which supposedly explains why revolutions in science and technology, unlike those in the humanities and some social sciences, have never posed a threat to the existing order (Harvey, 1973). The separation from politics which the natural sciences strove to maintain over centuries and which the humanities and the social sciences were never able to enjoy is no longer tenable.

Enhanced Social Accountability
Given what has just been said the contrast between pre-social science and pre-scientific humanities is breaking down. Mixed arenas have emerged in which natural scientists, social scientists, humanists and activists of all sorts are publicly debating issues that no longer respect the traditional boundaries between natural sciences and the humanities. The arguments between, for example, nuclear engineers and environmental scientists are suggestively similar to the controversies between enthusiasts for political correctness who object to the domination of literary studies by dead white male authors and those who insist that a great-and-good canon must be preserved and a back-to-basics cultural literacy promoted. Both are examples of the contextualisation of knowledge. Both reflect the confusing and contradictory pressures of social accountability – the former the increasingly precarious balance between the risks and benefits of scientific-technical progress, and the latter the changing demographics of mass higher education. Both, finally, demonstrate that under Mode 2 conditions the pressure for social accountability leads also to a shift in a criteria of quality. Quality in the humanities can no longer be determined largely by academic or other expert communities but must be validated against more diverse, and diffuse, external criteria.

Transdisciplinarity
Another Mode 2 characteristic, transdisciplinarity, is also endemic in the humanities, largely because arts disciplines have always lacked the robust construction typical of the sciences. The latter, under Mode 1 conditions at any rate, have been sharply delineated by highly specific techniques, often backed by complex instrumentation. Philosophy, history, literature and the others are much more loosely organised, professional microcultures held together by intellectual affinity but also marked by contradictory, even conflicting, interpretative communities. A distinction has been drawn between areas of contextual imperative and areas of contextual association (Becher, 1989: 89–90). The humanities are ordinarily found in the latter group. As a result disciplinary frontiers have always

been permeable in the humanities. Examples of transdisciplinarity and permeability are easy to find. The study of the classical world, once the property of philologists, historians, archaeologists and specialists in Greek and Latin literature, has been transformed by the insights of anthropology and the techniques of science; philosophy, generally in the diluted form of ethics, has spread across most of the applied social sciences; and cultural studies, urban studies, women's studies are emerging eclectic clusters of transdisciplinarity.

Instrumentation
Other Mode 2 characteristics appear to apply with less force to the humanities – which is relevant to the argument that it is the clustering of such characteristics rather than their individual effects that creates the conditions for the emergence of a new paradigm of knowledge production. Perhaps, after all, the humanities are an exception. Certainly, for example, the role of instrumentation seems more peripheral, although computer and other forms of information technology have come to be widely used in history (cliometrics), literature (concordance programs) and other arts disciplines. But at this stage it would be difficult to argue that these techniques are transforming academic practice in the humanities. Most scholars continue to operate in a traditional artisan fashion, the influence of information technology (IT) confined to the word-processor and fax machine! But, there have been other, more dramatic uses, of IT. Consider the way it was used to break the research practices of the few who sought to control, some thought in an overly restrictive way, the diffusion of the text of Dead Sea Scrolls.

However, the application of computer technology to the organisation of qualitative research in the social sciences, a process largely mechanical but with intriguing intellectual reverberations, has begun to spread to the humanities. It is through the computer's ability to assist with the construction of theoretical models, as in linguistics and to relate evidence to such models in a far more effective and systematic way, that the most significant impact of IT on the humanities is being felt rather than through the direct application of computers to scholarship by creating more comprehensive datasets though these are considerable and growing.

In a wider sense, of course, instrumentation has been decisive in shaping, creating even, the culture industry. Just as the invention of printing in the fifteenth century transformed the social contours and intellectual possibilities of the early modern world, electronic communication is reordering contemporary society, qualitatively as well as quantitatively. The aesthetics, as well as the accessibility, of culture have been transformed by these new technologies. The shift from theatre to films and television, and from concerts to records, tapes and compact discs, is far more than technology-assisted audience enlargement. Instead, performance, a unique event, becomes a product that can be endlessly reproduced. Culture is more thoroughly commodified. The economy of symphony orchestras depends on their recording sessions more than their platform appearances, which may merely serve as marketing opportunities.

Not only is the economy of the culture industry radically influenced by new technologies; not only, as a result, are individual aesthetic responses reshaped in ways which appear to undermine Kant's belief that aesthetic judgements are able to mediate between the objective world of science and the subjective world of morality; but the very idea of literacy itself is transformed. Visual sensibility and oral skill are clearly likely to be more highly prized than literary merit when telecommunications and IT permit instantaneous face-to-face interaction, the global village of the headline-writers. The 30-second soundbite is mightier than the elegantly drafted minute; the television documentary more persuasive than the finely written essay. Because all the humanities in their different ways are organised around notions of literacy, they are deeply implicated in these shifts, which have been produced by new patterns of instrumentation. Perhaps the anxious and awkward debates about the literary-philosophical canon, a core curriculum for the humanities, remedial courses and similar issues in the context of teaching, and in the research field the popularity of deconstruction and other forms of critical theory, and the rise of post-modernism, reflect these radical shifts in the idea and practice of literacy.

Reflexivity
Reflexivity, which has been identified as a key characteristic of Mode 2 knowledge production, has always been a traditional characteristic of the humanities in the sense that their intellectual energy comes from ceaseless interrogation of the past by the present. History, is constructed entirely on this premise, that without the past there can be no present except a featureless instantaneity. But literature, philosophy and most other humanities disciplines are as completely, if less literally, implicated in the same project. However, reflexivity gives rise to even more complicated and ambiguous effects in the humanities than science and technology.

First, out of this interrogation of the past by the present, if it is not pursued with rigour and integrity, can come a demoralising relativism. The alarming tendencies in modern societies towards narcissism and atomism, the decline in civic participation, the increasing sense that all relations and commitments are revocable, and the growth of increasingly 'instrumental' attitudes towards nature and society are all manifestations of a slide to subjectivism to which modern culture is prone. The social contextualisation of the humanities, now more explicit and insistent than ever, carries with it this danger, although some would describe such contextualisation as reflexivity run amok. In its most radical and theorised form, as postmodernism, it can even be carried to self-contradictory extremes. If all is incoherent and unconnected, playful shadows, how is reflexivity possible? Here a key dilemma is encountered, felt more acutely perhaps in the humanities than in science and technology. On the one hand reflexivity requires rootedness, a context in which and on which it can act. In modern society the links between agents and structure may be loosening, freeing individuals from the constraints of social class identities or prescribed workplace and gender roles and enabling them to modify these constraining structures through their own reflexive behaviour. But individualisation, and reflexivity, remain grounded in particular, if now more volatile, contexts. On the other hand, reflexivity appears to demand an ontological insecurity, an institutionalisation of doubt, the need to disembed intellectual forms from 'the immediacies of context' (Giddens, 1990). All givens must be mistrusted because they represent the treacherous reassurances of tradition which inhibit reflexivity. All utopian prescriptions must be denied – because they foreclose future reflexivity which, by definition, must be endlessly open-ended. Even science, even Reason, are suspect. Proof, after all, is terminal.

A second effect can be traced back to the acceleration of the culture industry and the apparently exponential growth of scholarship in the humanities. Put simply, the press of secondary works is so great that primary production is overwhelmed. According to George Steiner, 'literate humanity is solicited daily by millions of words, printed, broadcast, screened, about books it will never open, music it will never hear, and works of art it will never set eyes on'. The risk, therefore, is that reflexivity becomes a vicious rather than virtuous circle, a narcissistic process that owes far more to the internal dynamics of scholarly production and professional formation than to any external forces, whether social critique or economic imperative. Steiner again – 'commentary is without end. In the words of interpretative and critical discourse book engenders book, essay breeds essay, article spawns article. The mechanics of interminability are those of the locust' (Steiner, 1989). The result of this proliferation of commentary is ambiguous. Within certain strains of discourse it represents a tightening of knowledge rules and eventually the establishment of new orthodoxies. But taken together these many voices provide a loosening of all rules of discourse, and make possible a heightened reflexivity. An analogy with science and technology can be seen in the transformation and relative loss of importance of the original producer in a knowledge intense process: in science and technology the scientist and the primary discovery are just one ingredient in the production of knowledge. In the humanities the original work of art or literature recedes in the face of the proliferation of commentaries.

Is it possible any longer to make a substantive distinction between the arts and the sciences in the context of knowledge production? Through their links with the culture industry the humanities now have a direct impact on the real-world economy. They also shape life-styles, values and the political culture. For example, advertising images manipulate life-styles which accelerate consumption patterns. It can also be argued that individuals, freed from collectively imposed identities, choose cultural habit, objects and references to construct their new reflexive identities. Certainly higher education is used in this way. It offers a form of social credentialisation which now challenges older hierarchical principles. As the humanities play a key role in both mass higher education systems, specifically, and in cultural sophistication, generally, they are deeply implicated in these developments.

Nevertheless the alleged exceptionalism, or deviancy which is continuously reasserted by some artists and scholars must be addressed. The historical record does not help to resolve this question. It is certainly true that, at any rate in the Anglo-American world, the humanities have often seemed to stand in opposition to what were seen as the alien and alienating values of industrial society. In England the descent is clear from Coleridge, advocate of a secular clerisy to replace a dying priesthood in the 1820s, to F.R. Leavis, author of the revealingly titled *Mass Civilisation and Minority Culture* published in 1930, and beyond. Thomas Carlyle, Matthew Arnold, T.S. Eliot – these totemic figures in literature and criticism, despite their different perspectives, seemed nevertheless to embody that anti-industrial ethos (Weiner, 1981). In the United States the descent from Emerson and Whitman through cultural currents on both left and right to today's politico-literary intellectuals is more muddled but remains suggestive. Romanticism and other intellectual movements in Europe, part of which were a reaction against industrialisation have also repeatedly asserted a different epistemological status for the humanities.

One tradition in the humanities has seen its goal as the conservation of 'being', or 'time memorialised not as a flow but as memories of experienced places and spaces' (Heidegger, 1959) – at the expense of 'becoming', the province of the progressive natural and social sciences. There is no reason to suppose that this role has been abandoned. Indeed the contrary may be true because at a time of social fragmentation and economic change the desire for stable values is most intensely felt. It may not be an accident that the large-scale deregulation of financial markets and the privatisation of large parts of the postwar welfare state during the 1980s, which created great turbulence, were accompanied by restrictive policies in the educational and cultural arenas which attempted to emphasise traditional values: in the United States the movement for cultural literacy; in Britain the imposition for the first time of a national curriculum in schools; and, even in socialist France, a modified return to older educational values packaged as Republican virtues. A less assertive manifestation of the same search for stability at a time of rapid change is the growth of the heritage industry. Ruins, like roots, are big business.

Contextualisation and Meaning in the Humanities

The scientific community and also its analysts have traditionally emphasised the relative autonomy and the functioning of science as a distinct subsystem of society. Largely accepted up to the 1960s, this has been contested ever since. It does not account well for the practice of science even in Mode 1, and it certainly does not obtain for Mode 2. It is significant that the humanities have never been characterised in this fashion. They are clearly not an autonomous subsystem, insulated from the rest of society. Indeed, it is their function to provide an understanding of the world of social experience, and they are valued for the insights and guidance we expect to be able to derive from them.

What is characteristic of the humanities, is not just that they exhibit reflexivity in a more radical and continuous manner than the natural sciences or that they are, in essence, contextualised. What characterises them is that their reflexivity is expected to carry meaning for the entire human experience, to enrich the domain of signification. In that regard, they differ markedly from the natural sciences.

The social sciences, which have developed since the turn of the nineteenth century, share with the humanities a concern for the inner workings of society and the generation of culture and meanings. However, their viewpoint has generally been more analytic, and their explicit function more oriented towards the construction of practical and technical tools to better understand and manage the increasingly disenchanted world that their descriptions unravel. To maintain their analytic and technical posture, the social sciences have generally tried to maintain a style of reflexivity which links with contextualisation in a consciously detached manner. Contrary to the humanities the social sciences attempt to stay intellectually aloof from the creation of values and signification embodied in cultural production.

Since the last century, it has been an option in the humanities, and a very tempting one for its practitioners of an analytic bent, to mimic, borrow or adapt the methods and attitudes of more obviously scientific endeavours in the social sciences, or even natural sciences. This is one of the reasons why even in the humanities Mode 1 knowledge production, with its emphasis on disciplinary boundary work and certification, remains currently very active. Nevertheless, Mode 2 continues to predominate. This is not only because of its fruitfulness for the advancement of knowledge. It also opens the possibilities to examine not only one dimension of social life but to cut across disciplinary borders which makes it the most rewarding approach in the search for meaning. Indeed this is why established social scientists, when they want to put in to meaningful perspective what they have learned from their more analytical and disciplinary endeavours, resort to the preferred genre of the humanities, and write an essay. Essays – one of the oldest forms of Mode 2 production – roam freely in the territories seemingly held by the specialisms, link together what otherwise would remain fragmented analyses; they are, at their best, an art form highly conducive to the construction and dissemination of meaning. In history, the *Annales* school exhibits many of the characteristics of Mode 2 knowledge production and is described in Box 4.2.

Box 4.2
The example of *Annales*

Perhaps the most influential historical journal of the twentieth century is *Annales* founded in the 1920s by Lucien Febvre and Marc Bloch. One reason for its influence is that it has nurtured a glittering school of historians. Febvre and Bloch, of course, remain its iconic founders. Febvre is best known for his study of the dark-age and medieval belief that kings could cure scrofula by touching sufferers, a belief anomalously maintained into the age of Enlightenment by the *ancien régime*. Bloch is most celebrated for his study of medieval society.

Their heir, also their near-contemporary, was Fernand Braudel, responsible above all for institutionalising the *Annaliste* tradition in the sixth section of the *École des hautes études* and other strategic centres of intellectual life in France. In this way the *Annalistes* triumphed over potential rivals, most notably those more traditional social and economic historians who looked to Labrousse for leadership and inspiration, and secured a hegemony over history in France which has persisted to this day.

Braudel was also responsible for exporting the *Annaliste* tradition to the wider world, in particular Britain and the United States. In this respect his powers of patronage and organising abilities were less important than his personal achievement as a historian. He is author of the magisterial two-volume *The Mediterranean World in the Age of Philip II*, in which the immemorial peasant world of the Abruzzi and the famous Christian victory over the Turks at Lapanto are set in the grand flow, the *longue durée*, of historical change; of the even grander three-volume study of civilisation and capitalism, which sweeps the globe, from the European heartland to pre-Columban America and the Ming and Manchu empires, across the span of four centuries from the fifteenth to the eighteenth; and of two volumes of a history of France sadly uncompleted at the time of his death. The *Annaliste* tradition has been passed down to a third generation of historians. Jacques Le Goff returned to Bloch's original preoccupation with the rhythms of medieval civilisation. Emmanuel Le Roy Ladurie, as the author of the bestselling *Montaillou*, a study of the Inquisition's inquiry into the Cathar heresy in the Pyrenean foothills, and of an equally novelistic account of the carnival in sixteenth-century Romans on the Rhone, became one of the leading figures in the France of François Mitterand and is now director of the Bibliothèque Nationale.

However intellectual charisma and institutional patronage cannot in themselves explain the eminence of *Annales* and the *Annaliste* historians. Its and their success are good examples of the flow of knowledge, or cultural, production in the humanities – but also an ambiguous example. In one sense *Annales* and its school are manifestations of Mode 1 knowledge, because they permitted the penetration of rigorous scholarship into hitherto neglected arenas and encouraged a social-scientific rather than literary-humanistic conception of history. Often this has had a hard scientific, even positivistic, orientation. It is largely through the *Annales* tradition that French historians learned to apply the perspectives of physical geography and demography to the study of the past (although, revealingly, this particular aspect of the tradition received much less emphasis when the influence of *Annales* spread across the Channel and the Atlantic).

In another sense the *Annales* school exhibits many of the characteristics of Mode 2 knowledge production. Its promiscuous attachment to the social sciences, not simply the classic social sciences like economics, politics and sociology but anthropology and even demography, is proof of its endemic transdisciplinarity. This is also reflected in the topics made popular by *Annaliste* preoccupations. Strange, even shamanistic, beliefs have been recovered as legitimate subjects of historical enquiry alongside the dignified routines of polite intellect. The emphasis on *mentalité*, the rediscovery of past patterns of thought (which, because of an equal emphasis on history's *longue durée*, are also likely to be present patterns), demand qualities of creativity and imagination which are perhaps close to the radical reflexivity characteristic of Mode 2. The novel-like quality of some *Annaliste* works is also not accidental. The idea of history as a story, in a naive sense, and as discourse, with all its poststructuralist baggage, has been rediscovered. Finally, the *Annales* school is fascinated by manifestations of popular culture, the magic hidden inside daily routines. All this represents a radical contextualisation of the study of history.

In a large part of the humanities, however, cultural producers, such as novelists or some brands of philosopher, do not have to make any detour to delineate and express meaning. They see it as the essence of their activity. For them, the distance between creation and contextualisation is minimal; the analytical posture, the keeping of a distance from social action and the creation of values, are unnecessary since analysis is married to the creative production.

This is why there have been many intriguing correspondences between the growth of modern culture and the transformations of industrial society in which science and technology appear to have been triumphant. These correspondences do not reflect causal determinisms, but they are more than simple co-occurrences; they are co-constructions of meanings and cultural symbols, in which the social reality of the time is critically mirrored and creatively metamorphosed.

In the mid-nineteenth century as industrialisation became recognised as irresistible and irreversible, a critical stance became possible, calling not for a reactionary restoration of the past, its values and older art forms, but rather looking forward to the consequences of the triumph of that irresistible process. This is when classical writing disintegrated, while at almost the same time the refined solidity of Ingres' neo-classical painting gave way to the impressionists' deconstruction of light and form – and of traditional definitions of an art object. In 1863 Baudelaire wrote: 'modernity is the transient, the fleeting, the contingent; this is one half of art, the other being the eternal and the immutable' (Baudelaire, 1972). A similar co-construction of meaning occurred in the early years of this century as Einstein overthrew the Copernican–Newtonian order in physics, when Picasso, Braque and other painters discarded representationalism in art, when the tonal system in music was abandoned by Schoenberg and others, and when Proust and later Joyce and Virginia Woolf experimented with new forms of the novel unconstrained by conventional notions of time construction.

The current postindustrial transformation of the economy is also echoed by what has been labelled postmodernism in culture and the humanities. However, as before, since there is no determinism, cultural activity gives rise to very different visions and responses. This is one of the reasons why attempts to subsume all these reverberations under the notion of postmodernism are at times very confusing. These different visions and responses are the forms that contextualisation takes in the cultural realm. There is no single locus where a global view can be had of the entire context. Indeed, the very notion of the context as given, existing out there and available for description is put into question. Certainly realities exist that one strives to understand, but the only way to access them is through contextualisation, that is by building linkages and sharing signifiers to delineate and make sense of them.

Some revel in this apparent fragmentation, in the multiplicity of contexts that might be produced by different contextualisations, as well as in the corresponding ephemerality of the postindustrial order. They want to mimic these qualities in history, literature, philosophy. The risk is that this merely produces 'a rubble of signifiers'. But this is unlikely to deter the adepts of this vision from pursuing the fragmented, since, for them, by definition, consistency is always overrated.

Another – and contrary – response has been an angry denial of complexity – what Habermas (1987) has called a 'neo-conservative leave-taking of modernity'. It is directed less at the unchecked dynamism of modernisation than at what has been lost in terms of the cultural self-understanding that modernity tried to bring about. Neo-conservative ought not to be taken as a characterisation applying only to the political right. On the left, parties claiming to embody the continuity of historical progress have refused to entertain any notion suggesting the opacity of history and the indeterminacy of futures.

The rejection of grand theory – of any totalitarian intent to produce an all-encompassing meta-narrative, the context of all contextualisations – has led to attempts to find intermediate intellectual niches rejecting grand narratives but still enabling purposeful reflection, and so action, within more limited arenas. Such an attempt to construct a 'knowable world from an infinity of possible worlds', corresponds to the attribution of meaning in the process of local contextualisation. This can lead to a slide into the aestheticised localised discourse, exemplified most famously by Heidegger. Very different is the reaction of groups who contextualise their visions and expectations through active involvement in public controversies on the environment and technological risks. Such actors often find themselves integrated in Mode 2 knowledge production. The intensity of the conflicts and the eventual societal outcome are a function of overlapping local contextualisations brought about by different groups of actors functioning in that Mode.

A fourth response also starts from the viewpoint that all grand narratives have failed, but that one ought not to be satisfied with the finitude of local reconstructions of meaning, that in any case remain highly suspect. It has been described as 'riding the tiger' of hyper-rhetoric, rather as Nietzsche did a century ago when he tried to grasp a fuller understanding of contemporary culture in all its complex dimensions even if such understanding must remain beyond our intellectual reach and carries the risk of opacity, obscurity and misinterpretation (Harvey, 1989). Spoken or written discourse may not be the most appropriate medium for this endeavour which, in the past four or five decades, has found its most effective manner to convey meaning in the visual arts, albeit in an often elusive or disconcerting manner.

To regard such responses as discrete and/or coherent would be a mistake. It also certainly would be misleading to suggest that they can be calibrated against the characteristics of Mode 2 knowledge. On the surface the humanities share most of these characteristics with science and technology, although some, crucially perhaps reflexivity, have different meanings and impacts. But whether in a deeper sense the humanities can be said to stand in the same relationship as science and technology to this new paradigm of knowledge creation, which itself is intimately associated with the emergence of a radical new socio-economic order, is more problematical. In some senses the humanities stand a little aside, as quizzical commentators who offer doom-laden prophecies or playful critiques, and as performers who provide pastiche entertainment or heritage culture as a diversion from threatening complexity and volatility. In other senses they are even more deeply implicated; through the culture industry they fashion powerful, even hegemonic images, and through mass higher education they play a direct part in the new social stratification.

References

Baudelaire, C. (1972) *Selected Writings on Art and Artists*. London: Penguin.
Becher, T. (1989) *Academic Tribes and Territories*. Society for Research into Higher Education. Milton Keynes: Open University Press.
Bell, D. (1979) *The Cultural Contradictions of Capitalism*. London: Heinemann.
Giddens, A. (1990) *The Consequences of Modernity*. Cambridge: Polity Press.
Habermas, J. (1987) *The Philosophical Discourse of Modernity*. Cambridge: Polity Press.
Harvey, D. (1973) *Social Justice and the City*. London: Edward Arnold.
Harvey, D. (1989) *The Condition of Postmodernity: An Enquiry into the Origins of Cultural Change*. Oxford: Blackwell.
Heidegger, M. (1959) *An Introduction to Metaphysics*. New Haven: Yale University Press.
Jenks, C. (1991) *The Language of Post-Modern Architecture*, 6th edn. London: Academy Editions.
National Science Foundation (1990) *Science and Technology Pocket Data Book*, Division of Science Resources Studies, Figures 31 and 32, pp. 42–3, Washington, DC.
Steiner, G. (1989) *Real Presences: Is There Anything in What We Say?* London: Faber and Faber.
UNESCO (1988) *Statistical Yearbook 1988*. Paris: UNESCO.
UNESCO (1992) *Statistical Yearbook 1992*. Paris: UNESCO.
Weiner, M.J. (1981) *English Culture and the Decline of the Industrial Spirit 1850–1980*. Cambridge: Cambridge University Press.

5
Competitiveness, Collaboration and Globalisation

Summary

In this chapter we put the growth of Mode 2 knowledge production in to the wider context of international economic competitiveness, collaboration and globalisation. With the spread of modernisation and of industrial capitalism beyond the United States and Europe to Japan and the new industrialising countries, the comparative advantage on which advanced industrialised economies rely depends increasingly upon their ability to reconfigure knowledge. The strategy adopted by advanced industrial nations and established firms has been to rely on technological innovation to counter imitation of existing production methods by countries with otherwise lower wages or a more favourable capital structure.

This strategy has put pressure on firms of how to maintain successive productivity gains. It has led, for instance, to the development of specialist items needed to complete the innovation process being often contracted out. Manufacturing technologies are transferred to low wage countries and advanced industrial nations can only maintain their competitive advantage by using resources and skills which cannot easily be imitated. This demand is met by new technologies which in turn depend on the generation of new knowledge. In order to be internationally competitive, mature and leading edge firms must constantly keep themselves up to date in terms of knowledge and have instant access to it. One reason why the maintenance of in-house research capability has become too costly is that firms are unsure about the particular knowledge they need; often, it could have been produced almost anywhere. Another important precondition is to have access to such knowledge and expertise, being able to reconfigure it in novel ways and offer it for sale. What is highly in demand therefore is specialised knowledge for the identification and solution of problems. Because knowledge production is by no means a global phenomenon, knowledge firms must keep access to global intelligence and the new key techno-economic paradigm is increasingly based upon information technologies.

We argue in this chapter that parallel to the diffusion of Mode 2 knowledge production, network firms, R&D alliances, high value-added firms and new interface relations between competition and collaboration emerge. Although these new organisational arrangements and the sectors they cover vary, two broad trends underlie them. The first is a reversal of a trend towards tighter management control of more factors of production. In the past, many firms tried to absorb elements that had created uncertainties in the production process. The reversal is illustrated by the rise of the network firm and its organisational method of operation. Hierarchical structures are being replaced by horizontal ones and in general, these arrangements encourage flexibility and adaptation to unforeseen events. The second trend is that firms have ceased to try to carry out all their R&D in-house and have opted for cooperation with other firms as evidenced by the rise of inter-firm alliances. They allow to cut research costs, facilitate fertilisation between research areas and help to set technical standards.

Such a new contractual environment built on networks and alliances can be said to stifle competition. In contrast, we maintain that competition is stimulated on a second level. Competition no longer solely takes place on the level of making products or providing services in order to increase market shares. Rather, competition in an environment of alliances and collaboration is shifted to a second level, where there is constant pressure to innovate. Competition becomes one between design configurations and the ability of firms to develop their potentiality, resourcefulness and creativity. The trend towards more collaborative patterns and new alliances is an outcome of the fact that created comparative advantage results increasingly from the creative combination of resources and resourcefulness. This means that the source of value-added lies in the precise form which the collaboration of groups and the experience and skills of its members take. In this sense, competition can be said to be founded upon collaboration, since market selection is identical to group selection. In forming alliances firms make strategic key choices. We explore some of these strategies in a number of illustrative examples.

In many of these cases the mobilisation of varied skills and perspectives in the solution of complex problems is being built around the clustering of information, computer telecommunication technologies. The information technology paradigm increasingly replaces the previous one, dominated by technologies and organisation of past production consumption. A new paradigm begins to emerge when the new technologies become pervasive enough to seriously threaten existing ways of doing. Following Freeman and Perez (1988), this is exactly what is happening with regard to the four profiles of the new techno-economic paradigm: its technological, knowledge production, skill and capital equipment profile.

Returning to the significance and extent of the globalisation of the economy, we see some paradoxical consequences as well as novel contingencies. Despite the emergence of a new intellectual division of labour in the wake of the widened capacity to use research and scientific knowledge produced elsewhere, the ability to engage in research and to utilise it remains highly unevenly distributed throughout the world. An actual increase of inequalities occurs also through the differentiating effects that globalisation has on the actual ability to participate in the consumption of scientific knowledge, advanced technological products and systems, which leaves many regions and countries locked out completely. In general, we hold that inequalities of distribution have become more marked in the course of the process of global diffusion of knowledge production. The ability to transmit information cheaply and almost instantaneously throughout the world does not seem to lead to a more equitable distribution of scientific competence, but rather to its concentration. The growth of inequalities can be traced to the combination of two in-built tendencies: one towards standardisation, the other towards diversification.

Other paradoxical consequences of globalisation can be seen from the ongoing discussion about the deskilling or skilling effects of new technologies. But technology by itself does not require more or less skills, since it can be adapted to different levels of skills. It cannot be overlooked, however, that a new division of labour is taking place between high technology countries and the rest of the world. The 'industrial divide' is merely being shifted to a higher technological level. This is in full evidence when taking a closer look at the case of developing countries. As the complexities of contemporary science and technology unfold, the proposed solutions to current shortcomings of development appear all the more simple minded. Evidence is mounting that societies that were successful in building up scientific and technological competence, did so within a broader context of raising educational standards, changes of values, including a positive attitude towards science and technology. Success is also linked to focusing on long-term benefits for all, rather than expecting science to offer short-term technological fixes to complex economic and social problems or merely to aggrandise the prestige of political leaders and their grand projects.

The growth of Mode 2 knowledge production is partly an autonomous development, reflecting the inadequacies of Mode 1. But it is also one element in a much larger set of changes accompanying the spread of modernisation beyond the United States and Western Europe to Japan and the new industrialising countries (NICs). These changes have emerged from the larger historical development of industrial capitalism and so are interrelated. But some are linked more directly to Mode 2 knowledge production. The prosperity of the advanced industrial economies relies on their capacity to create comparative advantage which in turn, depends upon their ability to reconfigure knowledge. Mode 2 can be observed in traditional firms as well as newer, high value, enterprises that form the core of the emerging knowledge industry. Both type of firm will be considered in this chapter.

Strains in industrial capitalism can be partly attributed to the increasing number of players in world trade – nations which have mastered the techniques of mass production and are able to sell their products in world as well as local markets. The success of these newcomers is evident from their shares of world trade. Their enhanced capability has intensified international competition, because previous market leaders attempt to regain lost, or capture new markets. The strategy adopted by advanced industrial nations has been to place increasing emphasis on technological innovation; that is, the application of new technology to manufacturing and through its products to the satisfaction of sophisticated user requirements. Established firms have relied on technological innovation to combat imitation of existing production patterns by countries with more favourable capital structures or lower wages.

As a result firms must become more R&D-intensive. R&D, however, is very costly. The cost of maintaining an in-house capability is prohibitive. Many firms, including market leaders, subcontract the development of specialist items needed to complete the innovation process. The subcontractors are left to bear, at least part, of the R&D overheads. The intensification of international competition has stimulated the producer services sector, which supplies all kinds of specialist knowledge, including hardware. Many manufacturing technologies are being transferred to low wage economies. Advanced industrial nations can only maintain their competitive advantage by using resources and skills in ways which cannot be so easily imitated. Value-added arises from investing in production workers, supplying them with the most up-to-date plant and equipment. Investment in new technology has been the main source of economies of scale and at the root of successive productivity gains. Competition and the increasing sophistication of producer and user requirements is threatening this economic order by calling for bespoke items at mass production prices.

This demand is being met by new technologies which depend on the generation of new knowledge. To compete in world markets mature, as well as leading-edge, firms must constantly add to their own stock of knowledge and have instant access to it. One reason why some knowledge is too costly to be generated in-house is that firms are unsure about the particular knowledge they need and another is that, even if they can identify this knowledge, it is often difficult to gain access to it. The knowledge they need could have been produced almost anywhere. The level of R&D a firm can support is a function of its size. Large firms can support large in-house research budgets. But they still have to establish regular links with a range of external knowledge sources to complement their in-house capabilities. One illustration of this is shown in the growth of collaborative publications in the pharmaceutical and chemical-pharmaceutical sectors in both Japan and Western Europe, as shown in Box 5.1. In knowledge acquisition, however large firms are not always at an advantage. Small, flexible and non-hierarchical organisations may be just as effective like the specialised knowledge producers described in the preceding paragraph.

Box 5.1
**Some trends in collaborative research involving
Europe and Japan**

Japanese and European companies in the pharmaceutical, chemical-pharmaceutical and electronic sectors publish substantial numbers of scientific papers. They increased their published output over the 1980s, despite the effects of recession in the first half of the decade (first column of table). They publish in similar scientific fields, and in both the pharmaceutical and electronic sectors firms have increased their degree of specialisation. Their research is equally basic except perhaps in pharmaceuticals where co-authoring conventions may differ between Europe and Japan, thereby reducing the apparent presence of firms in more applied clinical research.

Collaborative research increased sharply over the decade,

How much did collaboration increase over the decade?

| | 1980–89 % increase in | | | % papers that are collaborative | |
	Total papers	Non-collaborative papers	Collaborative papers	in 1980	in 1989
Pharmaceuticals					
Europe	73	29	144	38	54
Japan	41	11	153	21	38
Chemical-pharmaceuticals					
Europe	12	-26	85	35	57
Japan	68	37	135	32	45
Electronics					
Europe	48	3	230	20	44
Japan	84	64	167	19	28
All sectors					
Europe	39	-3	133	31	52
Japan	69	45	156	22	33

as is clear from the table. Columns two and three address the question: which component increased – collaborative or non-collaborative paper publications? In every case, the number of collaborative papers increase far more than non-collaborative publications. Only European chemical-pharmaceutical companies did not at least double their number of collaborative papers. In contrast, the number of non-collaborative papers published by European chemical–pharmaceutical and electronics companies decreased or remained approximately static. The largest increase in non-collaborative papers was 64 per cent – in the case of Japanese electronics companies. Yet even this is less than the smallest increase for collaborative papers.

What fraction of the companies' research efforts are devoted to collaborative research? The last two columns in the table report the percentage of total papers that are collaborative. In both Europe and Japan, chemical–pharmaceutical companies collaborate most, followed by pharmaceutical companies, with electronic companies collaborating least. Japanese companies began the decade collaborating proportionally less than European companies (22 per cent compared with 31 per cent). By the end of the decade there was a substantial gap in all sectors, with European groups collaborating on between 44 per cent and 57 per cent of their papers and Japanese groups collaborating on 28 per cent to 45 per cent of their publications.

Source: Hicks et al., forthcoming

Access to knowledge and expertise, reconfiguring it in novel ways and offering it for sale, are becoming specialised functions and new mediating organisations are being set up to fill this gap. The demand is for much more than data or information, however technical it is, for knowledge, for the identification and solution of problems. Specialised knowledge is a crucial source of value-added even in mass produced products. Because knowledge production is now a global phenomenon, knowledge industry firms need to have access to global intelligence.

These firms do not use knowledge merely to solve problems, they also generate it in Mode 2. They employ problem identifiers, problem solvers and problem brokers. Their raw material is the global scientific and technological communities, regardless of whether these communities operate in Mode 1 or Mode 2, or are among the growing number of sites of knowledge production. Their success depends on the full utilisation of state-of-the-art information technology. The demand for specialised knowledge requires increasingly sophisticated means of communication and data processing. This, in turn, stimulates the microelectronics, telecommunications and computer sectors. This demand is leading to a profound structural change in the economy and industry. The new knowledge industries are the key to a new techno-economic paradigm – the information technology paradigm. The shape of this new paradigm is not yet clear. In this chapter only those elements of the new paradigm which appear to bear directly on the diffusion of Mode 2 knowledge production will be discussed: network firms and R&D alliances, high value-added firms, interface between competition and collaboration. Rising factor costs and intensifying competition – exemplified in the growth of the number of active partners in world trade – promote cost and risk sharing schemes among firms, leading to network firms and R&D alliances. These firms and alliances in turn stimulate the growth of enterprises designed to identify problems involving specialised knowledge. These enterprises which make up the knowledge industry, are crucial sources of high value-added on which national competitiveness and prosperity depend. Mode 2 knowledge production is deeply implicated in the emergence of this new techno-economic paradigm leading to a radical shift in the structure of institutions to meet the new requirements of knowledge production and distribution.

Networks Firms, R&D Alliances and Enterprise Webs

Over the past decade firms in many countries have formed new alliances. Although the details of these agreements and the sectors covered have varied, two broad trends can be identified. The first is the reversal of a trend towards tighter management control of more and more factors of production. This tighter control over the firm's internal and external environments was thought to lead to increased profits. So firms tried to absorb elements that had created uncertainties in the production process. The second is that firms have ceased to try to carry out all their R&D in-house and opted instead for collaboration.

The reversal of the first trend has led to the network firm. This type of firm exports costs by subcontracting activities to other independent firms, or handing over formerly internal activities to quasi-independent units. These activities may be in manufacturing (for example, making components, etc.) as well as services (for example, maintenance and cafeteria services). The economics of network firms depend on a trade-off between the lower costs of internal operations and the increased cost of managing an increasingly complex organisation. Spreading fixed costs between firms and their new partners leads to improved profits. However this process cannot be seen simply in terms of conventional subcontracting. In network firms the hierarchical relationship inherent in subcontracting is replaced by a medium-term cooperative and links between partners which are set out in detailed agreements. Similarly, hierarchical structures characteristic of the integrated multinational corporations are being replaced by new, horizontal relationships. The efficiency of these relationships depends on communication networks and well worked out, standardised, management principles (just-in-time stock control, etc.). These arrangements encourage flexibility and adaptation to unforeseen events even though the core corporation coordinates the marketing, and even the final assembly of products. The growth of new types of firms to supply specialist services, products, and advice of many kinds is encouraged

Network firms are popular in mature industries where competitiveness is largely based on lowering fixed costs. However, the spread of robots, flexible manufacturing plants and the substitution of economies of scope for economies of scale also encourage their growth. The popularity of network firms is likely to increase as products become differentiated and the pressures of uniformity slacken. Also local partnerships may make it easier for firms to adapt to demand and come to terms with many different and complex environments.

The move from vertically to horizontally integrated organisations is also reflected in the growth of inter-firm alliances. Such alliances are not based on the desire solely to externalise costs, but also to cooperate with other firms on common programmes. R&D and technology generation are especially likely to be the subject of alliances. There are several reasons for this: rising R&D costs, the search for cross-fertilisation between research areas and the need to set technical standards. Because alliances require reciprocal access to the R&D capacities of partners firms have had to change their behaviour. Traditionally, R&D has been closely controlled by corporate headquarters because it generated new ideas for future products and processes. With the growth of alliances, permeability is increasing. Flows of technological knowledge between firms are becoming more common. Even if individual transfers are closely controlled and limited to pre-competitive research, alliances involving cooperative R&D programmes help to open up internal corporate markets. This opening up remains restricted because knowledge flows only take place between members of the club. But as the number of clubs increases so too will the density of communication between firms. These two strategies – the formation of network firms and R&D alliances – are not incompatible. The same firm may externalise some of its mature operations while simultaneously establishing high technology alliances.

These two strategies can be seen as ways to avoid the most devastating effects of cut-throat competition. But more is at stake than self-preservation. In a global economy where knowledge is increasingly the commodity being traded, a new contractual environment built using networks and alliances may be necessary to stimulate competition. Alliances, because they are more or less transient, encourage the endless configuring of knowledge and so promote diversity within the economic system. Diversity stimulates rivalrous behaviour which, in turn, strengthens competition. The apparent paradox – that collaboration stimulates competition – can only be resolved by clarifying how alliances, particularly R&D ones, function.

Two Levels of Competition
The paradox of using collaboration to promote competition takes place at two levels. The first level of competition is among products for market share. Every firm employs a particular process technology to make products or provide services in order to increase its market share. High quality products and services, embodying more characteristics than consumers are being asked to pay for, and more efficient production methods, which permit prices but not profit margins to be reduced, are the dominant elements of competitive advantage. Further, every business stands in a hierarchical relationship with its competitors. Its overall competitive position is measured by its distance from the average performance of the competing group. Product quality and unit cost together define average performance at a given time. Above average businesses expand their market share; below average businesses stand to lose their market share, if they do not change their ways. How rapidly relative position can change depends on the properties of the market and the propensity of its competitors to expand. Firms with a static technology cannot hold their market positions and unless their market is sheltered they will not survive for long.

The second level of competition is created by the constant pressure to innovate. At this level competition is in turns of design configuration and the ability of a firm to develop its potentiality. It is about creativity and resourcefulness. Were this not so large firms would always dominate the innovation process. By improving its technology a firm is seeking to change its relative position in the competitive hierarchy. To maintain market share it must keep pace with improvements in average practice. Competition is like a race in which the finishing line is always receding.

The ability to innovate continuously is crucial to long-term performance. It is the source of creative comparative advantage which drives forward changes in terms of products on the first level. On the first level competition is concerned with technology, on the second level with knowledge and skills.

Created comparative advantage results not only from resources but from the creative combination of resources and resourcefulness. The novel element is that the relevant resources are increasingly human ones and widely distributed. The trend towards alliances is a natural outcome of the need to access these human resources. Resourcefulness consists in the ability to configure these resources and the source of the value-added lies in the precise form of the collaborative groups and in the skills of their members.

Competition on the second level is founded upon collaboration. On this level market selection is group selection. Competitive advantage for the individual firm depends upon the group it is in and this would change if the firm moved to a different group. In forming alliances firms need not be the only actors. They may co-opt other resources and competencies such as government laboratories, research institutes and university research groups. In forming alliances firms are in fact making key strategic choices. They are making judgements about the knowledge and skills which will be most important to their long-term performance.

The choice of a design configuration is among the most important that any firm ever makes. Increasingly the choice is of partners. The growth of technology alliances and pre-competitive research reflect the fact that each design configuration requires a range of resources whose precise character will be unique. Collaborative R&D is an example not of market rigging or anti-competitive behaviour, but of the dynamics of group selection. The problem is not one of replacing competition with collaboration but of managing the transition from one level to another and back again. The collaborative pre-competitive research produced by alliances provides an excellent example of Mode 2 knowledge production. This was the case with the search for an architecture for the fifth generation computers orchestrated by the Alvey programme in the UK , or the equivalent ICOT programme in Japan. In these programmes the search was on for a fundamental design configuration which would guide a whole series of further developments. Each included experts from industry, government research establishments, as well as universities. Each set the agenda which would occupy leading researchers in computer science, electrical engineering and mathematics. As the design configuration emerges one may expect to see not only a transition from collaborative to competitive modes of behaviour, but also a reconfiguration of individuals into a succession of new teams.

Collaborative ventures are partly defensive innovations in that they are aimed at reducing or sharing risks and costs. They are also offensive innovations in that they extend the skill base of the firm and the range of knowledge available to it and thereby improve its ability to compete. Because specialist knowledge is produced, collaboration can be a source of sustained competitive advantage because it is difficult to imitate.

The role of specialist knowledge is particularly evident in the development of producer services which many believe will become the prime source of sustained high value-added to sectors as different as high fashion and motor cars. In each case the producer services sector uses specialist knowledge to provide solutions which give products, even mass produced ones, their specific market edge.

Companies in the producer services sector are organised differently from those in mass consumption sectors. They have no need of either the large investments or the hierarchical organisations employing large numbers that have characterised mass production industries. Indeed, such large scale operations are inimical to the sorts of communication upon which mutual learning occurs and problem solving skills develop. In the producer services sector, data, information and knowledge are the principal commodities traded. By continuously reconfiguring these elements these firms are able to add value to a variety of other products and processes. Their competitive advantage lies in their ability to do this not just once, but again and again.

When the locus of value-added shifts from the creation of knowledge to its configuration, new types of productive workers must emerge to keep the process going. The groups that will give these firms their value will be problem solvers, problem identifiers and problem brokers (Reich, 1991). The form of organisation in which they will be most productive will not be hierarchical. It will have the capability to handle high density communications.

The producer services firm, then, takes on some of the characteristics of a spider's web. Each node is a problem solving team possessing a unique combination of skills. It is linked to other nodes by a potentially large number of lines of communication. To survive each firm must be permeable to new types of knowledge and the sector as a whole becomes increasingly interconnected. The interconnections embrace not only other firms but many other knowledge producing groups, be they in government research laboratories, research institutes, consultancies or universities.

The growth of the producer services sector illustrates the importance of specialist knowledge to all sectors of manufacturing industry as well as the new forms of organisation and types of skill required to capture the benefits that customised knowledge has to offer. The producer services sector is one element of an emerging knowledge industry. In this industry, knowledge information and data are the principal commodities being produced and traded. Its competitive advantage lies in the ingenuity with which its firms are able to reconfigure knowledge on a recurrent basis.

The success of the knowledge industry depends on the extent to which it is supported by an information technology infrastructure. This new infrastructure depends upon innovations in the telecommunication and computer industries that will make possible the ever closer interaction of an increasing number of knowledge centres. This new infrastructure is being put in place. Its effects will be pervasive and may in time lead to a new techno-economic paradigm.

We drew on the work of Chandler (1990) to illustrate the importance of three types of investment in the genesis of industrial development in the early and middle parts of the twentieth century. In brief, these were investments in technologies capable of yielding economies of scale in production, in distribution, and in the management systems that would make both operate efficiently. This approach to manufacturing is sometimes called mass production and it is paradigmatic in the sense that it sets up a general framework for all production activities and their management. This paradigm was diffused initially within the United States but much more widely after the end of the Second World War. One of the implications of the paradigm seemed to be a trend towards increasing bureaucratisation of production. As more and more aspects of production and distribution fell under the management imperative, so the size of organisations increased leading in the end to a degree of horizontal and vertical integration and subsequent growth in power that Galbraith (1969) felt could only be adequately described as the emergence of a new industrial state.

Yet, it is in the nature of all systems that unchecked growth in a particular dimension eventually becomes dysfunctional, and this, in turn leads to different modes of behaviour. In the late twentieth century some limits of the mass-production/-consumption paradigm have become most evident in the ability of low wage economies to imitate advanced production systems and in the increasing demand for bespoke products. Currently, new forms of enterprise have begun to flourish with the particular purpose of supplying established manufacturing firms with much needed specialist knowledge, what are sometimes called producer services. Producer services are fast becoming a (some believe, *the*) principal source of high value-added in advanced industrial societies. The point is that the modes of organisation, the management, and the skill requirements of the services are very different from those which have characterised similar activities in the past. In particular, high value enterprises do not need to control the vast resources that were characteristic of some of the earlier forms of mass production. To be effective producer services do not need to be organised in large bureaucracies employing disciplined armies of workers following inflexible, technologically- determined routines. Indeed, many would argue that in fact high value enterprise cannot be organised in this way.

The emergence of producer services represents in our view the early stages of what may one day become known as the knowledge industry. In this industry, data, information and knowledge are the principal commodities that are traded and the value-added, or competitive edge lies in the creativity to configure knowledge resources over and over again. When the emphasis thus shifts from the creation of knowledge to its configuration new types of productive workers must emerge to drive the process. Reich has identified the groups that give the new enterprise most of its value-added as problem solvers, problem identifiers, and strategic brokers. The form of organisation in which they will be most productive

124   *The New Production of Knowledge*

will be characterised by low hierarchies and a capacity to handle high density communications. Accordingly, 'messages must flow quickly and clearly if the right solutions are to be applied to the right problems in a timely way. This is no place for bureaucracy' (Reich, 1991).

Most importantly for our purposes is the description of how knowledge is created in these organisations. It is worth quoting at length because it describes very well, though in another context, what we mean by knowledge production in Mode 2. Creative teams solve and identify problems in much the same way whether they are developing new software, dreaming up a new marketing strategy, seeking a scientific discovery, or contriving a financial ploy. Most coordination is horizontal rather than vertical. Because problems and solutions cannot be defined in advance, formal meetings and agendas will not reveal them. They emerge instead out of frequent and informal communications among team members. Mutual learning occurs within the team, as insights, experiences, puzzles and solutions are shared. One solution is found applicable to a completely different problem; someone else's failure turns into a winning strategy for accomplishing something entirely unrelated. It is as if team members were doing several jigsaw puzzles simultaneously with pieces from the same pile – pieces which could be arranged to form many different pictures.

Whether you are talking about a project at the forefront of science (the human genome project), technology (fifth generation computer architecture), or a high value enterprise, the organisation that carries it looks less like a pyramid than a spider's web.

Strategic brokers are at the centre, but there are all sorts of connections that do not involve them directly, and new connections are being spun all the time. At each point of connection are a relatively small number of people – depending on the task, from a dozen to several hundred. If a group was any larger it could not engage in rapid and informal learning. Here individual skills are combined so that the group's ability to innovate is something more than the simple sum of its parts. Over time, as group members work through various problems and approaches together, they learn about one another's abilities. They learn how they can help one another to perform better, who can contribute what to a particular project, how they can best gain more experience together. Each participant is on the lookout for ideas that will propel the group forward. Such cumulative experience and understanding cannot be translated into standard operating procedures easily transferable to other workers and other organisations. Each point on the enterprise web represents a unique combination of skills. Enterprise webs come in several shapes, and the shapes continue to evolve. Among the most common are: independent profit centres, spin-off partnerships, licensing, and pure brokering. The threads of the global web are computers, facsimile machines, satellites, high-resolution monitors, and modems – all of them linking designers, engineers, contractors, licensees and dealers world-wide. (Reich, 1991: 91 ff.)

This description shows very clearly the centrality of specialist knowledge in the production process and the need for very different forms of organisation to capture the benefits that this knowledge has to offer. We have described this development in terms of the emergence of a new industry to highlight the fact that in it knowledge will be the principal commodity that is handled and traded and as such it will require a new cadre of skills to make it function. New types of organisation and styles of management are required by high value enterprises. In particular, they are intrinsically global and will become more intensely interactive as the telecommunications web diffuses.

The Information Technology Paradigm

The development some 15 years ago, of network firms and alliances presaged a radical shift in knowledge generating activities. In R&D alliances as well in the high value-added enterprises, scientists, technologists, engineers and social scientists bring varied skills to bear on complex problems. Their competence is measured by the contributions that they make to providing solutions, with disciplinary orientation and institutional affiliations less important. The mobilisation of these varied skills and perspectives in the solution of complex problems is being built around the clustering of innovations in information, computer and telecommunication technologies. This information technology paradigm increasingly replaces one dominated by the technologies and organisations of mass production and consumption.

What is involved in a change of a techno-economic paradigm? First it involves a shift in the basic approach of designers, engineers and managers to solving problems pervasive in all sectors of the economy. Second it rests on the universal and low cost availability of a new key factor in production. For example, the key factor was cheap steel from the 1880s to the 1930s, cheap oil from the 1930s to the 1980s, cheap microelectronics currently. Third, before a new techno-economic paradigm can generate a new wave of economic activity, a crisis occurs in the old. The old institutions which were adapted to an increasingly obsolete technological style tend, for a time, to lock out alternative systems. After a period of mismatch between a new technology and the old framework. A new paradigm begins to emerge when the new technologies become pervasive enough to seriously threaten existing ways of doing things. Currently the information technology paradigm, is based on a constellation of new industries which are among the fastest growing in all the leading industrial countries. In this case industries such as computers, electronic components and telecommunications, have already demonstrated a drastic fall in costs and a counter-inflationary trend in prices as well as vastly improved technical performance. This technological revolution is now affecting all other sectors, not only particular products, processes or services but also the organisation and structure of their firms and industries.

According to Freeman and Perez (1988) any techno-economic paradigm can be described in terms of four profiles: technological, knowledge production, skill and capital equipment.

Its technological profile comprises the capability for more rapid changes in product and process design; the much closer integration of design production and procurement functions within the firm; the reduced significance of economies of scale through dedicated capital-intensive mass production techniques; the reduction in the numbers and weight of mechanical components in many products; the more integrated networks of component suppliers and assemblers of final products and the potential for related capital saving.

Its knowledge production profile includes the growth of new producer services to supply manufacturing firms with new software, design, technical information and consultancy; and the extremely rapid growth of many small new innovative enterprises to supply these services and new types of hardware components.

Its skill profile reflects a change from a concentration on middle range craft and supervisory skills to both higher and lower qualifications, and from narrow specialisation to broader basic skills for information handling. Diversity and flexibility at all levels substitute for homogeneity and dedicated systems. Software design and maintenance become key skills everywhere. The deep structural problems involved in this change are now evident in all parts of the world. Among the manifestations of the shift towards the Information Technology paradigm is a persistent shortage of high level skills associated with the new paradigm, even in countries with high levels of general unemployment. In the early 1980s studies in many different OECD countries reported persistent skill shortages in software design and development, systems analysis and computer engineering. If anything these problems have become more acute with manufacturing firms in both Japan and Britain complaining of poaching by the service industries.

Its capital equipment profile also exhibits radical change. Computers are increasingly associated with all types of productive equipment as in computer numerically controlled (CNC) machine tools, robotics, and process control instruments, with the design process through computer aided design (CAD), and with administrative functions through data processing systems, all linked by data transmission equipment. The levels of global industrial automation expenditure in 1991 are summarised in Box 5.2. Computer-based capital equipment already accounts for between a quarter and a half of all fixed investment in plant and equipment in the USA and other leading industrial countries.

Box 5.2
Global industrial automation expenditures: 1991

*Current US$ billions and percentages of industry gross fixed
capital formation (gfcf)*

	Values	Percentage	Share
United States	40.0	29.9	20.9
Canada	3.0	2.2	9.5
Mexico	1.1	0.9	–
Latin America	1.6	1.2	–
Australia	1.1	0.8	–
Japan	27.3	20.4	–
Korea	2.9	2.1	–
Singapore	0.6	0.5	–
Taiwan	1.3	1.0	–
Hong Kong	0.2	0.2	–
Other Asia	3.1	2.3	–
France	6.9	5.2	14.5
Germany	16.5	12.3	19.6
Italy	6.4	4.8	–
United Kingdom	5.7	4.3	13.2
Other Western Europe	8.2	6.1	–
Eastern Europe, Russia etc	6.9	5.1	–
Middle East, Africa	0.9	0.6	–
Total	**133.9**	**100.0**	–

Source: Automation Forum (1993). Automation investment comprises
CAD/CAE, computer-aided production equipment, automated material handling test, inspection, communications and control, and
software. Share of industry gfcf calculated by OECD.

As a result of these changes and the problems they engender, there is a
growing search for new social and political solutions in such areas as
flexible working time, re-education and training systems, regional policies
encouraging information technology replacing tax incentives to capital-
intensive mass production industries, new financial systems, the
decentralisation of management and government, and access to databanks
at all levels. But so far, these are only partial and relatively minor changes.
If the Keynesian revolution and the profound transformation of social
institutions during the Second World War and its aftermath were required
to unleash the postwar wave of growth, then social innovations on a much

broader scale are needed now. This applies especially to the international dimension of world economic development and the telecommunications network.

Many of the changes that have occurred can be understood in terms of a much larger social transformation in which the emergence of Mode 2 is but one element. This transformation presents a number of paradoxes. These in part reflect the fact that appropriate institutions are not yet in place, but also reflect new problems arising from the new information technology paradigm itself.

Some Paradoxical Consequences of Globalisation

The significance and extent of the globalisation of the economy has been much debated. Similarly, questions have been raised about the extent to which firms draw knowledge from sources world-wide in their R&D strategies and whether this has any influence on where their R&D is actually carried out. There is some evidence, for example, that wherever multinationals may draw their information from, their R&D is still carried out locally – that is, in the home nation, so to speak (Patel and Pavitt, 1991). To some extent, doubts about the extent of globalisation stem from the fact that the needs of specific sectors differ and, therefore, what is an appropriate global strategy for one sector need not be for another. It also may be that the particular development characteristics of the electronics industry, which was globally oriented from the beginning, has been overrated. None the less, the knowledge industries are growing in significance for most manufacturing sectors, and for them at least the sources of knowledge production are already globally distributed.

To date, much of the debate about the activities of multinational firms has been concerned with the social, economic and political difficulties of their physical location. For many countries the location of plants is the primary consideration. They are perceived as a catalyst for a stream of further investments that will create jobs and initiate the process of industrialisation. But as competitiveness drives value-added in the wealth production chain in the direction of knowledge production, it becomes increasingly clear that to have a factory on your territory is, in itself, no guarantee of economic acceleration. Indeed, it could be the reverse.

Competitiveness and globalisation involve a double contingency. The first concerns the emergence of a new international division of intellectual labour as a consequence of the fact that, now, many more countries and firms have acquired the capacity to use research and scientific knowledge produced elsewhere. Science has always been the most international of activities. Despite this feature, the actual ability to engage in scientific research is unevenly distributed throughout the world. As with production, scientific research undergoes constant shifts in international competitiveness, with new countries entering and old dominance patterns breaking up – see for example, the growing pre-eminence of India in software design and engineering. There is clearly a relationship between excellence in science, especially basic research, and international competitiveness in production, but the relationship is not linear or direct. To be a leader in science is neither a necessary nor a sufficient condition to be pre-eminent in producing technologies for the world market. As recent studies have emphasised, the skills and knowledge developed in the context of basic research are equally important in the innovation process (Pavitt, 1991, 1993; Williams, 1986). Equally important, in addition to supply side factors such as investment in research and human resources, are demand side factors such as growing levels of disposable income which promote consumption and social experimentation with new products. Supply and demand factors together determine overall productivity growth.

The second contingency is related to shifts inherent in the globalisation of production and its differentiating effects on the production and use of scientific knowledge. While science is international, its funding mechanisms are still national. Although there is a marked growth in international scientific co-operation, mostly because no country can afford to finance the largest scientific projects alone, and although scientists are among the most internationally-minded and mobile workers, their career paths are still overwhelmingly shaped within the context of individual countries. Technology and production are proprietary in nature, whether their ownership is national or multinational, but consumption of scientific knowledge and of advanced technological products and systems, is a function of the level and distribution of overall economic performance. Countries that perform well economically are the more likely to be consumers of the most advanced scientific knowledge. Conversely, the inability to participate in consumption leaves large regions or countries locked out of the action.

There is little novelty in identifying competition as a force which leads to the concentration of wealth in the rich countries but it is not yet clear that globalisation is reversing this concentration. The convergence between science, technology and consumption has contributed to the spiral of economic growth. But while it has brought in its wake the global diffusion of knowledge production, the inequalities of its distribution have become more marked and visible.

There is an unresolved tension here. The changes in the balance of power globally and the consequent reconfiguring of economic units imply both that the component parts of the world economic system become both more, and less, dependent on the system. More, because a higher level of skills and knowledge will be needed to manage complexity; less, because management capabilities will spread more evenly.

But those changes are also threatening for many regions of the world. As the products of world-wide competition penetrate everywhere and countries are swept up into its vortex, local industries may lose their markets and traditional craft skills their status; the attendant concentration of knowledge and resources may make their research and teaching establishments appear irrelevant to the tasks in hand. Attempts by countries to protect their institutions, industries, farmers or workers by closing their frontiers and their minds to what is going on globally would launch them into a cul de sac. This is but one illustration of the potential volatility of environments which has been discussed previously. Still, what are the alternatives?

The conventional answer which would be to lower all barriers to trade and competition seem naive. Many countries believe that such policies will not bring results in an acceptable time and, understandably, resist them. Different strategies are possible. Consider for example the Asian Tigers, or what is being done for the integration of the economically less favoured regions in Europe into the European Union. The general rule seems to be that the successful enter the turbulent world of international competitiveness with a good safety belt on. The safety belt often takes the form of government agencies committed to long-range planning and institutions capable of long-range, non-profit- or low-profit-oriented financial commitments.

Still, the advantage does not lie unequivocally with large-scale enterprise. Other possibilities arise because the vortex of competition and concentration reaches only some segments of contemporary life. Outside of them, there is still a space for the small firm, the freelance specialist, the mobile and versatile person. Side by side with large-scale, standardised production and consumption, there is a growing market for personalised service, customised products and local initiative.

Growing Inequalities and Concentration
The ability to transmit information cheaply, and almost instantaneously throughout the world, does not seem to be leading to a more equitable distribution of scientific competence; rather, it is increasing its concentration. It is analogous to what happens when new highways link modern cities to less developed regions. The most able leave these regions, old leadership loses prestige, local industry is killed as mass-produced goods arrive by the truckload. In time, some jobs for unskilled activities in trades and services appear, and later, eventually, in some parts of the productive system; later, usually much later, scientific organisations and institutions are themselves put in place. In practice, the full development sequence seldom materialises. Those not associated with the main lines of development, it seems, are all too frequently marginalised. The globalisation process is extremely effective in destroying local cultures and organisations, but its

protagonists are, at best, uncertain as to how to replace them with truly functional alternatives.

These inequalities are due to the combination of two tendencies; one towards standardisation and the other towards diversification. This tension is well exemplified by the publishing industry and the mass media. The publishing industry in industrialised countries depends today on a small number of bestselling books sold in millions through thousands of standardised outlets, and supported by elaborate and expensive merchandising. Local newspapers struggle to survive and are being replaced by national and international magazines. In radio and television local stations join national and global networks, and reduce local programming to a minimum. Bestselling books, newspapers and magazines tend also to restrict themselves to a narrow set of issues, and the views of relatively few 'personalities', creating a provincial world on a global scale.

But, modern communications technologies are driving an opposite trend. Personal computers have turned small-scale publishing into a very affordable activity, cable and satellite television threaten, at both ends, the monopoly of national television networks, and the lower costs of communication allow information to flow simultaneously in all directions. The tendency towards concentration is compensated by diversification and increasing complexity. These tendencies will coexist: on one side are the small, increasingly complex and diversified communities of producers of modern technology and consumers of its more sophisticated products; on the other side is the much larger community of consumers of its more or less standardised products.

A similar situation exists in the practice of science itself. Computer networking makes it as easy to participate in collaborative scientific projects from a remote place in Latin America or Asia as from Boston. The lack of good libraries and journals, a chronic problem in less developed regions, will progressively be alleviated, as remote access to integrated databases improve and fax transmissions become cheaper. But negative side-effects ought also to be expected. Scientists and technologists from peripheral areas or institutions will experience pressure against working in native languages, or on questions different from those attracting attention in the main centres. They will be measured against their peers in these centres, not against those in their own institution or region (Goonatilake, 1984). There will be less reason to spread human and technical resources geographically.

More and Less Skills

The complex products of modern science and technology are becoming more user-friendly. There are two conflicting interpretations of this trend (Adler, 1992; Braverman, 1974; Senker and Beesley, 1986). One is the theory of deskilling, meaning that, as knowledge becomes more concentrated, labour becomes less qualified. The evidence for this can be seen in the growing utilisation of cheap, disciplined workers, usually young women, in the ubiquitous assembly lines of less developed countries that produce the sophisticated products in electronic and other high technology consumer goods. Further examples can be found in the various *maquiladora* industries in Mexico which reproduce a pattern widely found in many Asian countries. The second interpretation argues that deskilling is a feature of the past. Contemporary industrial production requires better educated and better trained persons, able to understand and carry on with their work in a comprehensive, rather than piecemeal approach. On this reading, countries which have kept alive an industrial craftsmanship tradition may still have a significant advantage particularly if they can support it with the latest in packaging and distribution technologies.

But technology by itself does not require either less or more skill. It can be adapted, often very precisely, to the level of skills. If the users and the workers are trained so that they have sophisticated skills, technology will be developed to make use of their ability. If they have very limited skills and competence, technologists will develop error-friendly procedures and routines. To some extent attitudes to technology are a function of its significance for the user. Automation is often regarded negatively when introduced on assembly lines. By contrast, in those professions (for example, medicine) where equipment is devised to enhance the use of knowledge and manual skills, status is not depressed and technology is regarded positively.

A new division of labour is taking place between high technology countries and the rest of the world. In the former the most complex tasks and highest profits are concentrated while routine and less expensive jobs are being diverted to the latter. This has been characterised as a new 'industrial divide' between those countries with a skilled population and an educational system providing the competencies needed to handle modern equipment and services and others constituting a world of consumers who learn only how to press buttons, and producers of standardised, low quality goods, whose livelihoods are continuously threatened by the advance of automation.

Complex Realities, Simple Solution: The Case of Developing Countries

The Second World War consolidated the belief that science was important, not only for winning wars, but in holding the key to future economic prosperity. Scientific research appeared to be a cornucopia open to all including developing countries. In order to tap the new resource – science – the United Nations, national foreign assistance agencies and private foundations from the industrialised countries supported the setting up of research councils in developing countries. It was generally assumed that with scientific institutions in place and given adequate scientific education, they too would become the beneficiaries of modern science and technology. This assumption has not stood the test of a grim reality. Not only did most Third World countries fail in their attempt to build modern, high quality scientific institutions, but even relatively well developed and well educated countries had to realise that their scientific and technological assets were insufficient if not accompanied by additional measures of support and policies.

As the complexity of contemporary science and technology unfolds, the proposed solutions to current shortcomings of development appear all the more simple-minded. Societies which were successful in building up scientific and technological institutions did so within a broader context of raising educational standards, promoting industrialisation, and the development of scientific, technological and managerial competence. Beliefs in the values of science and higher learning could not be taken for granted, but had to be instilled. Scientific, technological and educational activities could not be regarded as concerns only for scientists, engineers and educators. In many developing countries science was seen in contradictory ways. Modern science either claimed disinterestedness in questions of profit and independence from government; focusing on long-term benefits, stressing its role as a source of knowledge for industry and the learned professions. But seen from the perspective of bureaucratic authorities and political elites, science was expected to offer short-term technological fixes to complex economic and social problems. It was possible to keep these contradictory images and expectations distinct as long as a belief in the general benefits of science and technology prevailed and the scientists' prestige gave them access to the public purse. In many developing countries the characteristics of Mode 1 knowledge production found a niche with the pace of scientific development being determined more by the indigenous scientific community itself than by being forced to adjust to external circumstances which often were not conducive to the application of science in context. In other developing countries science and technology were put under close government supervision and developed for military purposes with comparatively little benefit for the general well being of the population. On the whole, those developing countries that were able to maintain more complex, multifaceted policies for science, technology and industrial development were more successful than those engaged mainly in ambitious, long-range and prestigious projects.

Government Policies and Private Initiative
The growing role of industrial and applied research in the context of a thriving business-driven knowledge industry may create the impression that public support of science and technology should be replaced by private initiative. The reality is much more complex.

Japan and the Asian Tigers, including South Korea, Singapore and Taiwan, are often presented as successful cases of free market economies. By contrast, state-driven economies such as India or Brazil are cited as having failed to be among the first of the technology-driven new industrially competitive nations. What such a comparison overlooks is the fact that the Asian Tigers have, until recently, been garrison states. They owe their economic achievements to existing close links between the public and the private sectors.

In contrast to the Asian Tigers, Brazil is often cited as an example of a country failing in its development drive because of excessive state interference in the economy. A brief description of Brazil's attempt to move to scientific technological self sufficiency is outlined in Box 5.3. Until the late 1970s, however, Brazil had one of the highest economic growth rates in the world. Its ability beginning in the early 1980s, to generate huge trade surpluses to pay for its foreign debt can be credited to the government's ambitious programmes of industrial and technological development a decade earlier. The reasons for the crisis and stagnation in the later 1980s are currently debated, with explanations ranging from the exhaustion of the import-substitution drive to economic constraints due to foreign debt, to the consequences of over-ambitious investments and a wasteful bureaucracy created during the two decades of military rule. It remains highly doubtful that the private sector alone will be able to replace the state in the drive towards economic readjustment and industrial modernisation including its scientific and technological base.

Box 5.3
From self-reliance to international integration

In the 1970s, Brazil embarked on an ambitious project of scientific and technological self-sufficiency. A university reform introduced graduate education and the organisation of universities in departments and institutes. Science and technology were important to the economic planning agencies, government investment banks and the military. New R&D institutions were created in the universities geared to research and training in advanced engineering and new technologies derived from recent advances in solid state physics and lasers; within the main state-owned corporations, in the fields of telecommunications, electricity generation and oil; and for agricultural research. A cooperation agreement was established with Germany for the development of nuclear technology. Several large military projects were initiated, including a space programme, with the development of launching vehicles and satellites; the construction of military aircraft; the development of a weapons industry; and the establishment of a policy of market protection for the computer industry.

In the mid-1980s, however, it was obvious that most of the hopes for social and economic development associated with this effort went unfulfilled, while countries with apparently much smaller scientific and technological capabilities, the so-called 'Asian Tigers', appeared as important partners in world trade, with significant benefits for the standards of living of their societies. This contrast has led to a large literature trying to explain what went wrong in one case, and right in the other. In hindsight, it is possible to point to some key factors that may explain some of the differences:

- The role of the State. In both cases the state was present in providing resources and devising policies. However, while in Brazil the government created its own industrial and research institutions, the Asian countries worked with incentives and coordination of the private sector. This association with the private sector forced governments to link their technological policies to macroeconomic considerations. In Brazil, long-term technological projects and short-term economic considerations were often at odds.

- Internal versus external markets. In Brazil, the effort was to develop a strong internal market of producers and consumers, before opening it up to international competition and try to capture a share of international trade. The Asian countries built their internal markets at the same time, in association with their growing interpenetration with the international economy.

- Trickle down versus building up. In Brazil, the expectation was that good academic science would lead to technology, high technology would lead to basic competence, technological competence would lead to industrial success, and elite education would lead to mass education. The Asian countries followed the opposite path. They started with basic competence, general education and the development of entrepreneurial skills, from which high technology, a skilled academic and industrial elite, and basic science are gradually being developed.

To cite an example of a developed economy – France is a country that in some of its government-driven sectors, such as computers, car manufacture and electronic consumption goods, has not become sufficiently internationally competitive. But other government-supported projects, such as the high speed train (TGV), part of the nuclear energy programme, and telecommunications, are unquestionable success stories both from an economic and industrial point of view. While these projects have been designed, financed and are carried out by large-scale state-run companies, the expertise of the private sector, a highly skilled workforce, and sometimes brilliant civil servants as managers, constitute an undeniable strength. The performance of government in economic development is ambiguous.

References

Adler, P.S. (1992) *Technology and the Future of Work*. Oxford: Oxford University Press.

Braverman, H. (1974) *Labor and Monopoly Capital: The Degradation of Work in the Twentieth Century*. New York and London: Monthly Review Press.

Chandler, A.D. (1990) *Scale and Scope: The Dynamics of Industrial Capitalism*. Cambridge, MA: Harvard University Press.

Freeman, C. and Perez, C. (1988) 'Structural crises of adjustment, business cycles and investment behaviour' in G. Dosi, C. Freeman, R. Nelson, G. Silverberg and L. Soete (eds), *Technical Change and Economic Theory*. London and New York: Pinter Publishers.

Galbraith, J.K. (1969) *The New Industrial State*. London: Penguin.

Goonatilake, S. (1984) *Aborted Discovery: Science and Creativity in the Third World*. London: Zed Books.

Hicks, D., Isard, P. and Martin, B. (forthcoming) 'An analytical comparison of research in European and Japanese laboratories', *Research Policy*.

Patel, P. and Pavitt, K. (1991) 'Large firms in the production of the world's technology: an important case of non-globalization', *Journal of International Business Studies*, 22: 1–21.

Pavitt, K. (1991) 'What makes basic research economically useful?', *Research Policy*, 20: 109–19.

Pavitt, K. (1993) 'Why British basic research matters (to Britain)'. Paper based on presentation in the ESRC Seminar Series: Innovation Agenda, made at the Institution of Civil Engineers, London 3 December 1992.

Reich, R. (1991) *The Work of Nations: Preparing Ourselves for 21st Century Capitalism*. London: Simon and Schuster.

Senker, P. and Beesley, M. (1986) 'The need for skills in the factory of the future', *New Technology, Work and Employment*, 1 (1): 9–17.

Williams, B. (1986) 'The direct and indirect role of higher education in industrial innovation: what should we expect?', *Minerva* 24 (2–3): 145–71.

6
Reconfiguring Institutions

Summary

This chapter deals with the process of institutionalisation under the conditions of the dynamics displayed by current knowledge production. The universities especially are at the core of present changes and strains since they still are the institutions mainly responsible for the training of specialists. We examine how the flexibility of Mode 2 knowledge production impinges upon their institutional structures and procedures, including the maintenance and change of quality control, how they cope with the strains of multifunctionality, what is entailed by what we call the pluralisation of the elite function, and finally, what the new institutional landscape of knowledge production looks like.

Knowledge producing, knowledge mediating and knowledge diffusing institutions have proliferated since 1945. Universities and university-like establishments of higher education, professional societies, governmental and corporate R&D laboratories, consultancy firms and think-tanks, nongovernmental organisations and other advocacy groups have multiplied and continue to create their own markets for knowledge. The most significant changes, however, are not connected with size, but with function. They have been driven essentially by developing links with new clients, reflecting the socially distributed aspects of Mode 2 knowledge production. The results have been a growth of multi-functionality. It is most acutely experienced inside the universities, but is manifest also in the increase of links across institutions and in networks of policy making and consultancy throughout. There has also been an emergence of new types of institutions. Examples include national offices of technology assessment and various agencies, boards and commissions of enquiry to carry out, monitor or assess environmental impact assessments. Many of these new institutions have been set up to improve the quality of public policy decision making and to manage controversies related to potential risks associated with technological developments. Other interesting examples are the small, hi-tech firms and the role they play in the increase of contacts between universities and industry.

Such institutional changes across a vast range of organisational arrangements cannot remain without repercussions for the individual scientist or practitioner of knowledge production. Their scientific career paths also are bound to undergo frequent changes. At the institutional level we observe a loss of clear-cut boundaries among the scientific elite and the rest. In connection with the diversification of funding, a complex, extra-scientific set of criteria related to social and economic as well as scientific priorities, relevance and accountability enters. The pluralisation of elite functions is enhanced by the intrusion of the market and the increase of both competition and cooperation in research. Under chronic budgetary constraints even the best institutions can no longer afford to do everything that seems best to them. On the international level, pluralisation takes the form of newly emerging patterns of both formal and informal cooperation, into which even the United States is drawn. Likewise, non-governmental international cooperation is on the rise. In general, faced with the necessity to reorganise the international division of labour, flows of knowledge, products, persons and ideas seem more important than structures. Doubts arise as to what extent national science systems have become dysfunctional and need to be overhauled.

The resulting new institutional landscape of knowledge production is marked by academic disciplines showing increasing fuzziness at their boundaries. In many areas and programmes, such as the Human Genome Project, transdisciplinary work has become the rule, but the same trend can be observed in the social sciences. Examples abound of 'real world problems' defying every attempt to be tackled by a single discipline. Interactions between science and technology and social issues have intensified. In some areas, demands for participatory science are articulated, where the goal is no longer truth per se, but responsible public decision making which takes inherent scientific uncertainties into account.

In the final section of this chapter we turn towards closer examination of three major challenges that result from the prevailing changes in the institutional landscape. They concern the management of disciplinary identities in trans-disciplinary settings and the development of transdisciplinary capacities; the challenge to universities and what successful adaptations to the new situations and demands could look like; and the new dimensions of quality control, since more diversified types of institutions imply a wider range of variety of standards.

The difficulties in setting up transdisciplinary institutional structures are well known. The fact remains that the disciplinary form of cognitive and social organisation is deemed necessary for providing a stable basic educational training and for instilling in individuals a sense of disciplinary identity. On the other hand, the capacity to cooperate with experts from other fields and to come to see problems in a complementary way, rests upon the capacity to assume multiple cognitive and, increasingly, social identities. Hence the necessity to find a balance to promote and to manage both. How deep the disciplinary interlinkages and genuinely transdisciplinary mode of working will go, depends on the nature of the research, the types of problems to be addressed and on the organisational context.

In turning towards the challenge to universities, one should not underestimate their capacities to change, despite the equally present evidence of inertia and outright resistance to change. After all, it is their monopoly of certifying competence which is being challenged by the emergence of Mode 2 knowledge production. While adaptations to the new demands and conditions are bound to vary, depending on history and circumstances, further change and diversification of both form and function appear a safe prediction to make. A crucial role in this process is likely to be played by governments themselves: everywhere they exert pressure to change, especially through new and tougher funding arrangements. At the same time governments recognise that traditional structures for knowledge production are not satisfactory, they also fear the loss of their own traditional forms of central governmental control. Finally, we resume the theme of quality control dealt with already in an earlier chapter. The reconfigured institutional arrangements which we described in this chapter imply that standards held by the various actors will enter the process of production and evaluation of outputs. It will also shape the decisions about what is to be done and by whom. Quality control will also assume a hybrid form.

Many academic scientists still hope that the changes in the institutional landscape will have a limited impact and that

**the number of new actors who have been drawn into the
process of knowledge production will remain small. Our view,
on the contrary, is that the present changes are too profound
and multifaceted. We believe that Mode 1 will eventually
become incorporated into Mode 2 knowledge production and
that the dynamics on which it rests will continue to unleash
further institutional changes.**

Knowledge is dynamic. New concepts, methods and instrumentation are
being continuously created leading to new capabilities and know-how, the
growth of new specialisms and increased division of labour. Though few
deny knowledge production possesses such characteristics, the current
understanding of the process assumes that development is linear and tends
towards stabilisation. Its dynamics are often depicted as a three stage
model of evolution, in which specialisation born in a discipline first takes
root in institutions and then becomes professionalised. This account is
favoured by those embarking on new areas of enquiry because it offers
their work appropriate recognition and creates conditions for long-term
support.

This chapter investigates institutionalisation, and asks whether the three
stage model is still a valid description of the way knowledge, particularly
knowledge at the forefront, is produced. Since it is the universities that are
mainly responsible for the training of specialists, it is necessary to examine how they are adapting their rules and procedures to the new
imperatives of knowledge production in Mode 2.

The traditional three-stage process is far from being the only, or even
the most appropriate, model. In contemporary knowledge production new
patterns of behaviour, organisation and institutionalisation are emerging,
better adapted to current and future social, economic and political concerns and needs. Because knowledge production is becoming more
dynamic and open-ended, its modes of organisation are less stable and
permanent.

The flexibility of the current mode of knowledge production does not
mean that former modes of institutionalisation are now obsolete, or that
anything goes. The urgent need for quality control of research results will
be discussed later. A function of knowledge institutions, evident in universities, is to enable specialisms to continue, to provide them with social
visibility and to legitimate them in the eyes of the wider community as
proper science. New forms of knowledge production are putting the existing institutional structures and procedures under strain, which require
new and radical transformations, especially in relation to the maintenance
of standards.

The Strain of Multifunctionality

The number and diversity of institutions devoted to knowledge production and dissemination has increased since 1945. In addition to universities and scientific and professional societies which have themselves multiplied, government research establishments have proliferated, corporate R&D laboratories have become a pre-condition for successful innovation and competition, think-tanks and all sorts of consulting firms and intermediary organisations, such as non-government organisations (NGOs) in the environmental field have emerged and created their own market for knowledge.

Increasing size has equally been a conspicuous characteristic of other types of knowledge production and dissemination institutions, governmental or private (for example, CERN, Bell Laboratories, or any number of government research establishments).

The most significant changes, however, are not connected with size but with function. They have been driven by developing links with new clients. They reflect not only the emergence of new fields, such as the environmental sciences or the health and social welfare professions, but also the rapid growth of continuing education in fields such as nursing, and management. New professions have not been accommodated by reduction elsewhere. New schools have been added, making most contemporary universities complex, multipurpose organisations. What is true of the institutions is true of their members. Not only are professors expected to teach and to do research, but they also have come to share a substantial part of the increasingly complex administration of their institutions. Consultancy has also grown rapidly. In the Netherlands most of the professors who are researchers of high calibre in the natural sciences and engineering are also consultants for industry. In most countries this is a growing trend, not only in the exact sciences, but also, though at a slower pace, in the social sciences.

Scientific and professional organisations, too, have expanded their functions. Many umbrella organisations such as the American Association for the Advancement of Science (AAAS), and also numerous disciplinary ones, have been created to promote the interests of various specialisms. Large, nationally-based professional societies in fields such as physics, chemistry or engineering, have long histories of involvement not only in university research but also as actors in the development of science policies, as guardians of standards of professional practice, as advisers to governments on a broad range of issues, as participants in public debates and in the promotion of the public understanding of science. Many individual members are directors of corporations or take part in setting national policies (fiscal measures, regulations, etc.). Many government research establishments now earn a growing fraction of their revenue by selling their expertise in the marketplace. Also numerous firms have developed professional training functions initially to keep their employees up to date with recent changes in technology or management, but later to provide these services to a wider constituency. This diversification in the functions of these organisations has increased the number of contacts between them, promoted the convergence of preoccupations and opened avenues for exchange and cooperation. A brief account of the efforts made by the National Science Foundation in the USA to accommodate the needs of new constituencies is given in Box 6.1.

Box 6.1
A new mandate for the National Science Foundation?

Walter Massey, President of the US National Science Foundation, has argued that his agency must move in a new direction; away from its traditional focus on investigator-initiated research towards broader social and economic goals.

According to Massey, the problem, in part, is chronic budget pressure brought about by the fact that NSF has so many different tasks to fulfil that there is now a mismatch between what the foundation is expected to do and what it can afford to do. Even before Congress cut the growth out of NSF's research grants in the 1993 budget, the agency was struggling to fund only about one-third of the applications that it received, though many of the rejected ideas were judged excellent by peers. But, according to Massey, the Foundation is also being asked to fund a portfolio of large instruments – such as radio telescopes, magnets labs, a laser gravity sensor – while expanding educational programmes and technology projects such as the high performance computing initiative: 'I don't think we can count on having the resource base' to support everything NSF is supposed to do 'with the rationale that we give now'.

Massey sees three alternatives into the future: cling to the status quo, reduce the agency's ambitions, or expand its role by promising to play an even more dramatic role in improving society. In his view, the first is not acceptable to Government, the second would effectively isolate NSF both from the mainstream of science and technology and from the public. He, therefore, prefers the third: a broadened mandate designed explicitly to boost US industrial performance and increase support for science. Yet this expanded mission, many scientists fear, would imply even greater extra sacrifices for basic researchers.

But both Massey and the members of Congress who shape NSF's future warn that reform is already on its way whether or not the agency welcomes it. The 1993 appropriations bill for NSF includes language from the Senate saying that the agency must concern itself more directly with the nation's economic strength. It demands that NSF draw up a new strategic plan emphasising a change in direction and not simply a wish for obtaining additional federal appropriations. Specifically their finance committees favour a reallocation of funds 'to strengthen certain priority areas: process research and development engineering research and emerging pre-competitive technologies and fundamental research with ties to future industrial interests'.

What many scientists see as a gamble Massey sees as political realism. He is simply responding to political pressures already evident from the committees that hold NSF's purse strings. They have told the NSF to pay more attention to research that will enhance US economic competitiveness. Even some of its staunchest supporters have been warning that it must find a new rationale if it is to maintain support from Congress.

For example, Congressmen such as George Brown argue that the need is for a fundamental reformulation of the principles of science policy. His committee – the Science Committee – stressed that the aim should be to exploit research as a tool rather than as a black box into which federal funds are deposited. The Committee talks about the need for 'performance assessment' to be carried out by persons or organisations independent of research performers. It may be necessary to establish a clear statutory mandate to redirect programmes that are not making sufficient progress towards stated goals.

Over 700 replies were received from individuals and organisations about the wisdom of Massey's idea of changing the basic charter of the NSF. Some organisations have responded positively:

Concern over technology application and competitiveness sometimes conjures up a choice that budgeting is decided on either the criteria to please scientists or to serve the public need. In reality these criteria and interests are congruent . . . the science and engineering community must better come to grips with the reality that many fields not covered by the traditional disciplines offer challenges for new knowledge and opportunities for creative investigative research worthy of the most gifted scholar. These fields should be valid candidates for support and may both yield key knowledge and enable timely response to national goals. (A Foundation for the 21st Century: A report of the National Science Commission on the future of the National Science Foundation, Nov. 20,1992)

Not surprisingly, many academics expressed concern: 'I believe that the very close symbiotic relationship between academia and industry especially within NSF, as favoured by Massey would be a disaster. It would shift resources toward the development of new technologies . . . This runs counter to the unique mission of NSF and I'm afraid that it would ruin the soup' (M.J. Greenberg, Director, The Whitney Laboratory, University of Florida).

Although this example is derived from the USA., similar, but perhaps not so radical, reforms are occupying the minds of policy makers in many countries and for the same reasons, rising costs of research coupled with severe problems of industrial competitiveness.

Source: Marshall (1992) © 1992 by the AAAS.

Finally, new types of institutions have appeared. Examples include national offices of technology assessment which began to appear in the early 1970s, or the various agencies, boards or commissions of enquiry established to carry out, monitor or review environmental impact assessments which in many cases are mandatory. These new institutions marry the expertise of the natural sciences and the social sciences in order to improve the quality of public policy decision making and to manage controversies related to risk and to the externalities of technological development. Another type of new institution is the small hi-tech firm. Their economic significance was recognised in the early 1960s and they have continued to play a decisive role in the development of the microelectronics, telecommunications and biotechnology industries. Small, hi-tech firms are distinct from other small firms because not infrequently they are spin-offs from universities or government research establishments. Even when they are not, they are generally associated with universities because of their need for high level consultancy, research facilities or trained personnel. In the United States, professors often sit on the boards of these small companies, thus enhancing the potential for genuine research collaboration. The close interaction between universities and small firms in research parks now plays a strategic role in regional development policies.

Levels and Forms of Pluralisation

At the individual level, the definition of what makes a good scientist is now much more pluralistic. The freedom of individuals, to make innovative choices, and design their own intellectual itineraries is sharply increased. But their scientific careers will undergo frequent transformations.

At the institutional level, other phenomena are occurring. Massification and the proliferation of functions have meant that not every activity carried out in elite academic institutions can be of the highest standard. Since it is no longer self-evident which institutions or centres have elite status, labels of excellence are coming to depend on the judgement of bureaucratic committees. This is closely connected with the dependency of institutions on external funding. Currently, success in attracting funds for research depends on meeting a complex set of extra-scientific criteria related to social priorities, relevance and accountability. Increasingly, the goals and requirements of programmes have made it unlikely that a single institution would qualify as a centre of excellence across the whole range of research inputs needed. It has become a common pattern for such centres to be created as multi-institutional units or networks, often with the more or less mandatory participation of industry. Such a trend also implies a dilution of the group of so-called elite institutions by including experts in not so elite institutions, thereby creating new patterns of communication, cooperation and dissemination.

This pluralisation of the elite function is a response to the intrusion of the market and the increase of both competition and cooperation in research. Institutions that want to remain elite are also forced to break long standing habits of allocating resources across all specialisms. Even the best institutions have to restrict the range of their activities. The best managed institutions respond by finding or designing market niches to exploit the specific range and competence, skills and knowledge they house. In so far as they act entrepreneurially they enter into, and try to anticipate, the behaviour of the market.

On the international level, pluralisation takes the form of newly emerging patterns of both formal and informal cooperation. Many formal international agreements have been driven primarily by cost-sharing considerations initiated by CERN-like arrangements. They have been followed by programmes which are national in the sense that they are financed and run mainly by researchers and administrators from one nation but have been deliberately opened to foreign collaborators to induce their governments into cost-sharing arrangements such as the Super-conducting Super-collider or the Human Genome Project. European countries, more than the United States or Japan, have in recent decades, in the context of the research programmes of the EU attempted to reap economic benefits by 'going international'. Small countries often turn to international cooperation as a way of overcoming the constraints of size and costs. But even the United States which has traditionally accorded low priority to international cooperation in science, partly because of its decentralised structure and partly because it has not been perceived to be vital to American interests, has now become much more active; for example, in using the forum provided by the OECD to monitor and coordinate the setting up of large, expensive facilities in basic research.

Perhaps of greater importance for the future is the growing non-governmental international cooperation on the informal level. The number of scientific papers co-authored by scientists from different countries is increasing rapidly. This is not only an aspect of globalisation, but also a manifestation of the increasing tendency to use knowledge, information, collaboration, wherever they may be found. Immediate access to knowledge is now more a function of networking and less of institutional position. Important computerised databases and on-line capabilities, as well as access to knowledge, remains very much a matter of personal contacts, and of extended, informal communication patterns. Here again, flows are more important than structures, and the challenge for institutions now is to find ways of supporting ever more complex and changing communication channels rather than to invest in costly, heavy and inevitably rigid forms of institutionalisation.

At a time when even nations in the forefront of science and technology cannot adequately fund all that needs to be done, could not the need for cost and information sharing provide the conditions for bolder thinking in international terms for more rational use of resources, by reorganising the international division of labour? The possibility of regional, or even global, universities combining research and teaching may point to interesting futures. Such universities would involve substantial exchange programmes for personnel – from national universities, industries and other research institutions – and students, and broad geographical distribution (the building of new campuses along the lines of the traditional forms of universities no longer seems the appropriate way to do things).

There are doubts as to what extent national science systems have become dysfunctional and need to be overhauled. Such doubts challenge cherished beliefs and dogmas, for example that only investment in a 'Western style' national science system can provide a country with its international competitive edge or that lack of investment or relative underspending in academic research provides a hidden subsidy to a nation's competitors. The home country of multinational firms is still a crucial factor in determining where the benefits of technological innovation will ultimately flow.

The combined force of the transformations occurring at the individual, institutional and international levels are also sources of stress. Researchers will be faced by an overload as demands generated by Mode 2 knowledge production are added to those produced by traditional forms of discipline-based enquiry. Professional identities are loosened and broadened, scientific careers become more precarious and mobility adds to strains already inherent in any scientific career.

The New Institutional Landscape of Knowledge Production

Specialisation was traditionally seen as a pure product of division of labour, as a consequence of an existing research activity evolving according to the internal logic of a discipline. The growth of knowledge produced within disciplines, and the ever proliferating problems emerging from new results, made it necessary for individuals to specialise. This process no doubt still obtains, but this is far from being a complete description of what is happening. This is why focusing exclusively on institutions rather than exploring the setting up of flexible communication channels would be a mistake. The production of new knowledge no longer occurs only inside disciplinary boundaries. It also occurs in the interstices between established disciplines, through the cross-fertilisation between disciplinary areas, and through the diffusion of instruments and procedures which affect the practice of research in often remote areas.

Disciplines show increasing fuzziness at their boundaries. New research endeavours, for example biotechnology, bring together biochemists, microbiologists and chemical engineers. The Human Genome Project requires cooperation of molecular geneticists and software experts. In such areas transdisciplinary work has become the rule. Molecular biology has not evolved according to the conventional disciplinary pattern because it has transformed the way questions are framed and research is done in immunology, genetics, or cell biology. Other new fields, such as risk assessment or technology assessment, remain areas of cooperation between experts from many disciplines. These hybrid and provisionally stable forms of knowledge, formed in the context of application unfold to perform specific jobs with agendas constructed in a complex socio-political process.

This trend can be observed in the social as well as the natural sciences. In the social sciences examples abound of 'real world' problems that clearly defy tackling by any single discipline. In policy work as well as in more theoretical investigations issues are arbitrarily defined when approached from a single disciplinary viewpoint. The creative challenges to the social sciences come from research perspectives or programmes which seek to be in closer touch with phenomena and problems found in the 'real world'.

One of the reasons why boundaries have become fuzzy and why

institutionalisation is taking new forms is related to the diffusion of Mode 2 knowledge production. In all realms of culture and society, the new mode is developing alongside Mode 1. As more and more aspects of life in society are perceived to involve issues having a techno-scientific dimension science cannot be left to scientists alone. The methods and techniques of knowledge production in Mode 2 have become important ways to investigate societal issues in which many individuals and groups have some stake. Examples of this are numerous: environmental and agricultural matters, diet and health problems, computerised databanks and privacy. Interactions between science and technology, on the one hand, and social issues on the other, have intensified. The issues are essentially public ones, to be debated in hybrid fora in which, there is no entrance ticket in terms of expertise. In such a participatory science, the goal is no longer truth per se, but responsible public decision making based upon understanding of complex situations where many key uncertainties remain to be resolved. New intermediary institutions are required to support this collective learning process, to manage interchanges between groups of interested parties, to analyse them, and to prepare the ground for decisions and to monitor and evaluate their results. These new processes are not under the control of scientific specialists, though the latter remain essential. Now specialists have a double responsibility. They have to be responsive not only to the scientific community but also to public decision makers.

Disciplinary Identities
Disciplinary boundaries matter far more in education than in research. They are more important inside the university than outside. Their strength and support rests upon the task of transmitting knowledge to the next generation of students. Departmental structures may become rearranged as is the case for the biological sciences, to follow the shift from Mode 1 to Mode 2. But there are no universally acknowledged principles about how to draw disciplinary boundaries. Criminology, demography, urban studies, geography, statistics, botany, plant biotechnology or operations research are recognised as disciplines in some universities and countries, but not in others. Disciplinary boundaries are the result of history, vested interest, financing, entrepreneurial opportunity or of academic coalitions.

   Even if the extreme disciplinary conservatism found inside many university structures were overcome by moving research outside universities and closer to real world problems, it is not obvious that by transferring research to new institutes, centres and units, a more transdisciplinary research mode would emerge. Experience shows, that in governmental laboratories set up for problem-solving and close interaction with industry, the internal dynamics of specialisation tend towards university-like rigidities. American universities have traditionally been more open and flexible towards the growth of disciplinary research centres than their

European counterparts. Much seems to depend upon the links between such transdisciplinary fields of studies and the larger, societal environment.

The difficulties in setting up transdisciplinary institutional structures are not merely a manifestation of inertia. The fact is that the disciplinary form of cognitive and social organisation generally deemed necessary for providing a stable basic educational training confers on individuals a disciplinary identity and a 'competence card'. Through their training, especially if it remains mono-disciplinary, individuals come to share a specific world view and learn to value what are considered significant problems, how they are to be framed and solved. Conformity is encouraged by disciplinary collegiality, by expectations and rewards from the disciplinary peers. The capacity to cooperate with experts from other fields, to come to see the world and its problems in a complementary way and to empathise with different presuppositions, involves the capacity to assume multiple cognitive and social identities. In some fields, such as the social studies of science and technology some researchers succeed in maintaining a double identity, being loyal both to the discipline they have come from and to the field of science and technology studies. Biologists working in environmental science, computer scientists in the analysis of gene sequences and mathematicians in ecological modelling can equally gain reputation on both their native and new grounds. Such options are, however, not equally available to researchers coming from all fields.

Policy makers believe that knowledge production can be speeded up by recourse to transdisciplinary thinking. They may be naive and underestimate the organisational as well as the subtle career-related impediments that, in practice, distort good intentions and correct insights. The demand for greater and faster solution power persists but the complete substitution of transdisciplinary for disciplinary forms of training is not practical. It is necessary to have a balance or sequence of balances to promote diversity between disciplinary identity and transdisciplinary competence. How deep the disciplinary interlinkages and interpenetration go depends as much on the nature of the research programme and the types of problems to be solved as on the organisational context.

A crucial aspect, however, is the time horizon appropriate for disciplinary work. The time horizon of a policy maker is almost by definition short. But disciplinary structures are long-term and relatively stable. To qualify as a biologist, physicist or economist, takes many years and marks one's self-understanding for a life-time, even if the actual nature of one's work undergoes considerable changes over the course of a researcher's life. Involvement in disciplinary work may be continuous, but it is more likely to be intermittent, and involve, as one moves from one problem to another, participation in a range of different teams. To contribute creatively – rather than merely engage – in the kind of cognitive and institutional pluralism which transdisciplinarity demands is a more arduous task.

The number of transdisciplinary endeavours is sharply increasing and more and more researchers, at least at some point in their career, become involved in them. The demand for this type of knowledge comes from policy makers, industry and society generally. It is now sufficiently developed to constitute a new type of market. New opportunities and funding are being offered to attract researchers who in turn are challenged to come up with ideas, products and proposals for solutions likely to find a customer.

Yet, a price must be paid if transdisciplinary research is to become the norm. World-wide interdependence of research and industrial innovation imply a degree of vulnerability for those who engage in research. It is most evident in those firms or sectors of industry approaching maturity. Firms trying to cope with competition at this stage often respond by internal reorganisation, in the nature, volume and composition of their research force. The need for rapid problem solving is interpreted by management as a need for transdisciplinary research. The most efficient way to achieve this is to recruit new research competencies. But, this is both costly and wasteful. This dilemma can be resolved by increasing the fungibility of researchers; that is, by moving scientists and engineers to new jobs demanding other skills and a different knowledge profile. Most firms do not possess the resources to do this. Instead they look externally for retraining. In some cases universities' extension programmes have provided some of the services needed. However, this remains mainly a domain for private organisations who find it easier to provide the kind of highly specialised customised training which is demanded by industry.

Disciplinary research has been associated with long-term modes of work and knowledge production. It has relied on a small number (say 5 per cent or even 15 per cent) of those who work at the cutting edge of knowledge production to provide the new ideas and directions of future research. This is a necessary but not a sufficient condition for scientific growth. In transdisciplinary research new seeds are constantly being produced which then need to be put into more stable 'furrows' to produce 'crops'. In policy terms the key questions are: How much stability, predictability and routine, is needed to support the more exotic, intermittent and transitory unstable patterns of transdisciplinary work? How much fungibility is possible? How much insecurity can individual researchers bear without their creativity suffering? The most practical answer is also the most general: adaptability is the condition for continuous success. An environment is needed which cultivates institutional openness and flexibility, and which allows room for experimentation and initiative in local arrangements.

The Challenge to the Universities
Most universities have changed enormously since the Second World War, before massification, the explosive growth of R&D spending, and the proliferation of new functions in the postwar decades. Indeed, universities have changed more in these past few decades than in the previous three centuries. We should not underestimate their capacities for change.

Nevertheless, their capacities for resistance to change are also formidable, rooted in the power of academic guilds, in their organisational arms, departments and disciplines – and ultimately in the traditional monopoly of certifying competence in defined areas of knowledge. That monopoly is being challenged by the emergence of Mode 2 knowledge production, close to the contexts of use. That challenge coincides with other strains on the university, arising out of massification, the most visible of which is the inability of funding sources to keep up with growth and the rapid increase in the costs of traditional forms of science. In the past, the growth of university budgets has supported change: new needs have been met largely by the creation of new kinds of institutions, faculties, departments and research institutes. Universities are now faced with more intense pressures for change, but under conditions of financial constraint. And the question arises in many countries: can both the old and the new universities adapt to the new demands and conditions? And what would successful adaptation look like?

The short answer to the first question is: yes, through further change and diversification of both form and function, and the surrender of their monopoly position in the world of knowledge production. They can, and in some places do, survive as one player, and an important one, in what is increasingly a distributed knowledge system involving many people and institutions outside the universities. We can already see the forms of successful adaptation as well as the results of the failure to adapt. In some cases powerful US research universities which have been leaders in traditional science areas retain that distinction in some areas while other of its members and units join the world-wide networks of Mode 2. In other, often newer segments of higher education, diversification is within a system of more internally homogeneous institutions, some of which maintain relatively stable research niches in particular industries, products or services. These institutions, whose research is already close to the contexts of use, will almost inevitably change with the nature of their markets. In those segments, marked by a division of labour between, rather than within institutions, the unit of adaptation is the system of institutions, as well as each of its members.

But while some colleges, universities and segments show a capacity for change, the needs of markets and users change faster than the capacities of most universities to respond. What we see is a shift within institutions towards the parts which are most adaptable – and which are nearer the contexts of use. In some countries this includes the professional schools, and most conspicuously, the engineering and medical schools, and schools of business, of management, and of public policy. The secret of adaptability is for at least some academics and academic administrators within a university to become part of Mode 2, to move inside the research networks and into the changing markets for goods and services existing outside the university. The test of institutions, and of governments, is whether they develop policies and structures which allow, and indeed encourage, this to happen.

The pressures for change arise not only from the changing modes of knowledge production, but also from all the agencies that have a stake in knowledge production, most particularly from governments. Everywhere they exert pressures for innovation and change on the universities. The results can already be seen in the establishment of new research centres, university–industry units. The creation of competitive segments of higher education intended to be more open and responsive, new and tougher funding arrangements, and new requirements for research assessment and accountability have been put into place or are under discussion. But those pressures are not always in the direction of adaptability and responsiveness; sometimes they merely increase rigidities in research agendas by strengthening the instruments of central control and management, substituting the decisions of ministers and civil servants for those of the traditional scientific community. Governments increasingly recognise that traditional structures for knowledge production are not satisfactory, but fear the loss of traditional forms of central governmental control inherent in the growth of Mode 2 knowledge production. Their special concern is loss of ownership of their universities which turn to the growing numbers of other clients – business and industry, regional and international organisations, citizens' groups, professional organisations – who make new demands on the universities but also provide them with alternative sources of financial support. Government policies will be successful to the extent that they recognise that the inadequacy of the traditional science research system does not call for yet another rigid research system designed by a ministry, closely controlled and monitored by central agencies.

New Dimensions of Quality Control
The diversification of institutions, the emergence of hybrid fora and the demand for greater social accountability raise, once again, the question of the management and control of quality in the knowledge production process. Diversification brings with it a collapse of monopoly power in quality control and a change in the criteria on which quality control is based. The terms of reference, and the common standards used, must involve broader criteria to reflect the nature and diversity of actors now involved. If no single authority can any longer exert quality control

according to its standards alone, then the reconfigured institutional arrangements – whether in the funding of research, or the evaluation of its outputs – imply that standards of various actors will enter the process and shape the decisions about what is to be done and by whom. Moreover, standards will have to be revised periodically as new interests or actors enter or established ones leave the quality assurance process. These changes, in turn, induce institutional flexibility. The overall result is a redefinition of standards and the formation of hybrid forms of quality control. This does not mean that 'anything goes' or that quality will be lowered. Rather traditional scientific criteria will have to be qualified by other criteria which can claim equal legitimacy. In very different hybrid fora standards and procedures of assessment will differ markedly. For any individual or collective actor the number of options will increase, regarding where they want to play and with whom.

This may explain a paradox in the behaviour of universities where individuals may be highly entrepreneurial but formal committee structures are stodgy, unimaginative and often unable to make decisions. Individuals have a wide variety of choices in which league they want to play, be it only on a very local amateur team. Provided they gain admittance they all have local or international contacts according to the options they choose, but the number of ways in which individuals can demonstrate comparative advantage is extremely large. This does not hold for universities, departments, or planning committees for whom the range is much more restricted and since there does not exist a well articulated market in which they could demonstrate performance. Because of this, evaluation criteria remain stereotypical, bearing upon the most traditional functions of universities, for example, teaching or long-term research. Consider universities which have a state-conferred monopoly on teaching: no matter what their other achievements their performance continues to be evaluated in terms of a single teaching standard.

Being able to choose in which game and league to play opens up not only many more possibilities for the individual or research group, but also makes the play a far more interesting one, since criteria can evolve in a variety of directions. Of course, to function properly some stability is needed; negotiations cannot be carried on indefinitely or be completely open-ended. Criteria for closure are necessary for the continuance of any social process. However, where the basis for quality control is narrow and slow to change, the range of status-conferring activities and, therefore, competitive potential are correspondingly reduced.

More diversified types of institutions imply a wider range of socially accepted behaviours, and a greater variety of standards. This further implies a greater number of cut-off points where performance is evaluated, and the outcome channelled back into the process. The system as a whole becomes more error-friendly, since failures can more easily be compensated for. Also, errors are noted more quickly and can be corrected more easily provided loose coupling is preserved. The outcome now depends on how efficiently corrections are fed back into the process. Compared with linear thinking and planning, institutional configurations of the kind discussed here, because of their greater flexibility, permit earlier and more efficient change of course.

Two knowledge producing systems – Mode 1 and Mode 2 – currently coexist. The key question is whether the current coexistence will last. Many academic scientists still hope that the changes in the institutional landscape which we have described have had a limited impact and that the number of new actors who have been drawn into knowledge production is still comparatively small. Our view, on the contrary, is that the present changes in knowledge production are too profound and multifaceted to make this a realistic expectation. We believe that Mode 1 will become incorporated within the larger system which we have called Mode 2 and other forms of knowledge production will remain dynamic.

Reference

Marshall, E. (1992) 'NSF: being blown off course?', *Science* 258 (5084): 880–2.

7
Towards Managing Socially Distributed Knowledge

Summary

In the final chapter we aim to address issues likely to be of particular interest to policy makers. In accordance with Mode 2 and its distributed character, the framing, definition and means for solving even what appear to be common issues, are also bound to be highly locally contingent. What may appear as the most pressing problem in one country, firm or university, might already have been solved in another instance. Means and resources as well as what counts as 'solution' will also differ. Solutions that appear to be similar may enjoy high legitimation and consensus in one place, but not in another. Therefore we refrain from providing specific answers even to questions which need to be addressed everywhere. We do highlight, however, six future issues at the very end together with an indication of the likely evolution of underlying trends.

Leading up to them, we take the interested reader through the main threads of the argument once more and attempt to locate it in the development of science and technology policy until now. We distinguish between three main phases, marking the transition of a policy for science towards science and policy and, during the 1980s, entering a policy for technological innovation phase. Our argument is stated as a plea for the initiation of a policy for distributed knowledge production, a policy that ultimately is people- and competence-centred. The policy to be developed will need a new management style, which can cope with permeable boundaries between institutions and other features of Mode 2 knowledge production. Governments and their agencies, alone or in cooperation with others, will do well to function as honest brokers. Much of the success of the new policy will depend on the ability to provide an adequate framework for the management of the distributed knowledge in flux and to better manage the interface between competition and collaboration on several levels and in different forms. Perhaps most

crucially the new policy will have to confront a potential
imbalance between volatility and permanence of the institutions involved, a middle ground between stable and flexible
forms of organisation.

The transformation of knowledge production, in the sense described
above, is one of the central processes characterising the societies of the
advanced industrial world. Knowledge production is less and less a self-
contained activity. It is neither the science of the universities nor the
technology of industry, to use an older classification for illustrative purposes. Knowledge production, not only in its theories and models but
also in its methods and techniques, has spread from academia into all
those institutions that seek social legitimation through recognisable competence and beyond. Science is less the preserve of a special type of
institution, from which it is expected to spill over or spin-off to the benefit of other sectors. Knowledge production is increasingly a socially
distributed process. Moreover its locus is global, or soon will be. At its
base lies the expansion of the numbers of sites which form the sources for
a continual combination and recombination of knowledge resources; the
'multiplication of the nerve endings of knowledge' that we have discussed repeatedly throughout this book. The expansion of the number of
sites where recognisably competent research can be undertaken has implications for the management of the knowledge production process and for
the maintenance of quality control within it.

The distributed character of knowledge production constitutes a fundamental change. To it are linked the other dimensions of change which we
have explored: the increasing contexualisation including the marketability of knowledge, the blurred boundaries between disciplines and
institutions and across institutional boundaries, fungibility of scientific
careers, transdisciplinarity not only of hot topics, increasing importance of
hybrid fora – groups constituted through the interplay of experts and non-
experts as social actors – in the shaping of knowledge.

The continuing massification of the university as a teaching institution
is a prerequisite for this wider distribution in society of the capability to
produce and use knowledge. But, as we have argued, some changes in
emphasis are necessary. In particular, students need to learn how to find,
appropriate and use knowledge that might have been produced almost
anywhere in the world. However, it is in the adaptation of their research
function to the distributed character of knowledge production that universities are most challenged. The university must enlarge its view of its
role in knowledge production from that of being a monopoly supplier to
becoming a partner in both national and international contexts. Such a
change will, before long, involve a redefinition of excellence among academics, of their career aspirations, of their disciplinary contributions, and

their institutional loyalties. The universities, in their turn, will need to explore strategies of niche specialisation.

In industry, too, the distribution of knowledge producing capability raises profound questions about the appropriation of that knowledge for its own purposes; that is, about the extent and organisation of industry's in-house R&D as well as about the ownership and management of intellectual property and acquisition of the skills needed to configure knowledge resources in a manner relevant to industry's competitive situation. Resourcefulness in the management of the configuration of knowledge is a precondition for success in a world where the intensification of competition in markets internationally, together with the transformation of the information infrastructure, have made technological innovation the name of the game.

This analysis of the transformation of knowledge production indeed entails major changes in the approach to policy. Although this volume has been concerned with knowledge production in its broadest sense, including the humanities, the changes in policy orientation that are now required can be seen more sharply by focusing on scientific and technological knowledge. Therefore, in this last chapter, we will explore the significance of the shift in the mode of knowledge production against the background of the development of science and technology policy over the past half century.

Our approach to policy issues is intended to be broad and heuristic. The trends that we have observed do not appear with equal weight in every country. Indeed, national trends in this regard reflect a particular institutional colouring of Mode 2 knowledge production, so that across nations unequivocal patterns are unlikely to emerge. However, a number of general issues arise as a consequence of the transformation of the knowledge production process, issues which policy makers from all countries will have to consider.

Three Phases of Science and Technology Policy

Much of science and technology policy is currently in the doldrums. Having gone through at least three phases of policy thinking during the last twenty years, the scientific community has had significantly to modify its approach to what is considered worthwhile in research. Policy thinking now seems to be intellectually exhausted as it moves towards yet another phase. Its characteristics grow out of the transformation of knowledge production, but they also reflect, and call into question the assumptions which have guided thinking in the earlier phases. For this reason it will be helpful to review, briefly, their main characteristics.

Policy for Science
In the first phase, the problem as expressed in the writings of Vannevar Bush (1946) and Alvin Weinberg (1963), among others, was posed in terms of working out a policy for science. The main issue, then, was the growth of the scientific enterprise per se. The key questions, then, were concerned with criteria for choice within science; setting up guidelines for choosing between expensive projects, often in different disciplines. This vision of science policy, in which the key decisions were to be taken by scientists, now seems untenable if not naive. None the less, it still lingers in the minds of many in academia as the norm of a proper policy for science. Such a policy, however effective it may have been, has now become inadequate. And that is because it addresses itself principally to what is happening within disciplines whereas the global dynamics of knowledge production have become much more concerned with what is happening outside or alongside them. So much is happening outside the traditional disciplines that it seems folly to formulate policy entirely from within them.

Science in Policy
In the second phase, both scientists and policy makers advocated a reform: policy needed to shift from policy for science to policy in which science was seen to support the objectives of other policies – a shift to science in policy. The Brooks Report (OECD, 1971), the Rothschild Report in the UK (1971), and the Research Applied to National Needs (RANN) programme in the USA, were examples of this new perspective. The intention was that science and technology should play a key role in achieving the diverse policy objectives of a modern industrial state rather than simply aiming at the development of science itself. Yet, in neither of these first two phases was much attention given to how science might contribute to national well-being. That there were potential benefits to be had from science was unquestioned, but it was not the scientist's job to extract them. In the event, deteriorating economic performance throughout the late 1970s and the early 1980s in virtually all industrial economies eventually forced a critical reappraisal of the notion of science as the locomotive of economic performance. This in turn, brought forth another policy shift.

Policy for Technological Innovation
During the 1980s, declining economic performance and increasing worldwide competition forced policy makers to narrow their perspective on the role of science in achieving national goals to the single question of how to hitch the scientific enterprise to industrial innovation and competitiveness. By means of a new range of initiatives aimed at promoting, first, strategic and, then, generic technologies, policies shifted to

technology as a more effective base from which to support national industry. In part, this was a response to falling competitiveness vis-à-vis Japan, but it also reflected the widespread belief that, at root, the technological base of the economy was depleted. It then became one of the aims of policy to repair these fundamental structural weaknesses by supporting the development of infrastructure technologies (for example, semiconductors, new materials, etc.). A strengthening of those technologies which underlay industrial competitiveness was felt to be needed rather than stimulating innovation through specific product and process developments. This change of orientation and belief clearly exhibits some of the attributes of knowledge production in Mode 2: a blurring of the distinction between science and technology, the creation of national (Alvey in the UK and ICOT in Japan), and in some cases supranational (ESPRIT and EUREKA) programmes in particular technological regimes built around configuring national resources, the establishment of networks and other informal modes of communication among the active partners and growing familiarity of university scientists with working in large, often multinational, teams.

At the moment, the impetus of these policies seems to be slowing despite, or perhaps because of, the fact that in many countries, particularly in the USA, productivity and, hence, international competitiveness has still not improved substantially. Throughout this period, the scientific communities in many countries have stressed the importance of basic science to industrial well-being. Industry, in its turn, under pressure of rising costs, has had to narrow its commitments to basic research. Currently, policy is log-jammed trying to maintain a creative tension between a vigorous scientific enterprise and the imperatives of competitive industrial structure. It is our contention that science and technology policy has been put into this quandary because its goals of policy have been broadened without questioning the fundamental presuppositions it entertained from the beginning. The question that has not yet been fully tackled concerns the contribution to economic performance that can be realistically expected from disciplinary-based sciences, institutionalised largely in universities, and driven, intellectually by internal considerations. These problems are now recognised but have not been solved because the underlying assumptions about the role of science in the economy have yet to be critically addressed.

Under these new conditions, science and technology policies (phases 1 and 2) and innovation policies (phase 3) can no longer be regarded as functionally separate. Indeed, this is already the case in many countries where, under the label, 'science and technology policy' or research policy, it is actually innovation policy which is being pursued. Generally, this is done with only meagre success because the presuppositions of older science policy thinking linger on and continue to structure the thinking of policy analysts and decision makers. In the new phase, innovation policy, if it is to be efficient, will supplant the older science and technology policy thinking. It will be a new type of innovation policy, predicated upon a broader understanding of the innovation process and of the constitutive role of knowledge and the knowledge producing institutions in it. A key element in this new understanding is already becoming clear. It is that people in their fungibility, multicompetence and capacity to connect with others are the crucial resource.

Policy problems cannot be properly addressed until policy makers take into account the many significant changes taking place in the production of knowledge, in industry as well as in the traditional sites where science is practised. The traditional approach has been to export the problem of deriving economic benefits from science and technology to the people who manage the interface between science and industry, leaving activities on either side of the interface largely unchanged. Ironically, this has occurred when many of these interfaces have become more permeable. This permeability has been brought about not by policy but because the best university scientists realise they need to interact more strongly with knowledge created outside. In the top-flight academic institutions the notion of technology transfer is giving way to the notion of technology interchange.

Rethinking Basic Assumptions

What does a policy for distributed knowledge production look like? It will require some radical departures from the traditional viewpoint.

First the notions of separate science and technology 'markets' have to be abandoned since actors do not move in accordance with linear, sequential and hierarchical models, step by step from research to development to innovation and use. Basic science has become inseparable from technological development linked by the innovative use of instrumentation. It has been conventional to view the frontier of science as expanding from the core of its activities. In the current context however, both core and frontier are spreading. This is evident is such areas as molecular biology, biotechnology, new materials, nanotechnology, liquid crystal and solid state physics, nuclear fusion, informatics and superconductivity.

Second the new policy models are no longer the 'systems' type popular a decade ago among policy analysts. Systems models imply greater stability in the relationships between actors than is justified given what we already know of distributed knowledge production. More helpful descriptions could be worked out by trying to develop models that incorporate the evolution of patterns of interconnections, the ability to establish, on a recurrent basis, new modes of exchange, the skills to adapt to the richness of research practice, and to create ever new channels of communication. Third, specialisation takes on entirely new forms. They are not to be understood as a further division of labour inside already constituted disciplines. The new specialisms which drive discovery and innovation are problem-oriented and mostly transdisciplinary in character. They break with the common vision of specialisation as an incipient discipline or subdiscipline that is starting on its way to professionalisation and institutionalisation. They exhibit much more mobility. They are tied to the resolution of clusters of problems and will develop in accordance with new problems.

The Management of Distributed Knowledge Production

The policy to be developed will need a new management style. The traditional approach – some variant on management by objectives like the systems approach – is too inflexible. The management of a distributed knowledge production process needs to be open-ended, and to break away from classical planning perspectives. The management of processes, particularly of the external environment becomes paramount. That management style can be summarised in two notions – increasing permeability of boundaries and brokering.

In distributed knowledge production the dynamics of science and technological innovation are the principal driving forces leading to the emergence of new forms of organisation. While some universities and research institutions have been slow to adapt, the best have already become more permeable and integrated into new networking arrangements. The process of increasing permeability of boundaries weakens the centralising tendency of bureaucracy. Policies of decentralisation should incorporate incentives to encourage openness and reward individuals who can achieve economies of scope with existing resources. Large university-based institutes with tenured faculty, or government laboratories for fulfilling specific functions as well as permanent research units with tenured research staff set up for specific monocultural research, will not be the policy models of the future. Such organisations have become too expensive and inflexible to meet the needs of distributed knowledge production.

An alternative model might involve the creation of lean 'centres', employing few administrators with a budget to stimulate networks of innovators, in units attached to diverse institutions, agencies or firms. They would be periodically evaluated in terms of their effectiveness in process management. When their jobs were completed, or when decreasing returns became evident they would be disbanded. These centres, like other institutions, created in the context of socially distributed knowledge production are likely to have many stakeholders and will need to be run and evaluated accordingly. Any policy that tended to entrench institutions, or encourage autarkic attitudes, is anachronistic.

It is well known how to set up laboratory sites to pursue scientific investigations of various kinds. We also know how to build teams around single professors and individuals of exceptional talent, for example, Max Planck Gesellschaft in Germany. What we do not know so well is how to manage the art of facilitating efficient communication between such nuclei as well as between the other equally important elements that one finds in Mode 2. This is a matter not only of facilitating relationships between groups of researchers but also of making easier communications with innovators, regulators, venture capitalists, etc.

The second notion in this phase should be for government, alone or in cooperation with others, or some of their agencies, to function as honest brokers. Governments are a logical choice for this role because much of the brokering is likely to involve other governments or their agencies. Brokering is necessary because in distributed knowledge production more actors, not all technical experts, are involved. Brokering will demand exceptional skills because the individuals involved in the innovation process will come from many different institutions and organisations, they will often be dispersed geographically and may only be able to work on a problem or project part-time. Distributed knowledge production is diffusing rapidly because congenial settings embodying a large variety of organisational styles are being established. The task of policy is to provide the framework for the management of this flux.

This implies that the policy arena itself will undergo a drastic change in composition. Indeed, this has already begun. During the phase characterised as policy for science, it was expected that academic scientists would be key policy players. This has become much less so, as governments have shifted from the support of science for its own sake towards innovation policy. During the last two decades not only politicians and civil servants, but economists, marketing experts and industrialists, have become involved in the genesis of science and technology policy. This intrusion of the wider interests of society is sometimes resented by scientists because it is felt to erode the independence of the 'Republic of Science'. But there are good reasons for the shift in the locus of authority in the development of science: it reflects the distributed nature of knowledge production.

Issues related to risks for health or the environment posed by technological development, or issues related to the impact of information technology on jobs, training and competence, or ethical issues brought out by new biomedical technologies, are becoming matters for public debate. In short, the new innovation policy is now, inescapably, a part of politics.

However, attitudes and processes characteristic of earlier phases of science policy will survive. We are describing not a historical break but rather a significant shift of emphasis. Some priorities will continue to be set within the scientific establishment – resource limitations will make this imperative. Also efforts will continue to be made within the scientific industrial system to filter science through the sieve of industrial needs. Arguments about priorities and about protecting the national science base will continue but the agenda is no longer being set primarily in universities or in national research councils. Though scientists remain the driving force in proposing areas for research, the research priorities will be generated within hybrid fora composed of many different actors. These priorities now have both a cognitive and a social dimension. Innovation policy will be concerned not with the details of this process but with the direction and support of the multiplication of knowledge production sites and the management of complexity that results from acceleration of knowledge interconnections.

This new style of management is not required simply because of the increase in the numbers of new sites of knowledge production. It is also necessary because of the transformed nature of the aims and content of knowledge production. The two processes are interconnected. The changing nature of what is regarded as important in science and the new requirements of its production have induced the organisational changes described before. The close interaction between form and content in knowledge production is the primary reason why the new tasks have become those of handling and processing knowledge. This requires new approaches to creativity, strategies for preserving and increasing the permeability of institutions, for designing and intensifying interlinkages among them, for managing flux rather than administering institutions old and new.

But all this rests ultimately on a policy that is people and competence centred. This new innovation policy will need different institutions, although some existing institutions will adapt more successfully than others to a new style of management. It will also require a new competence to create and design, rather than to reproduce with marginal improvements. This is one of the reasons why we stress the importance of developing policies that promote interchange among scientists and technologists and the general connectivity of innovation systems, possibly using information technology to exploit its knowledge base. The competence – the new skills and perspectives that emerge from these interchanges – is at least as important an outcome of this mode of knowledge production as the problems solved or the artefacts created. This implies policies that promote transdisciplinarity and provide for the possibility that unusual modes of organisation may be required; policies that promote international collaboration and that seek to be aware of, and be able to interpret, knowledge wherever it may be produced. In managing this flux, people as the carriers of competence will constitute the main resource.

The new policy will also have to manage better the interface between competition and collaboration. Managers of innovation policy will need to shift continuously back and forth between competition and collaboration. The job of governments, of research managers and others is not to pick winners, whether individual products or generic technologies, nor simply to create an environment which encourages rivalrous behaviour. So far international competition occupies centre stage in most national innovation policies and will continue to do so for the foreseeable future. Competition generates diversity by provoking rivalrous behaviour among the competitors. In the production of knowledge this implies the ability to experiment. Dynamic competition is essentially a discovery process – it leads to innovation. But innovation also reduces diversity and rivalry can become dysfunctional. It is the function of collaboration to restore diversity. Rivalry itself is not enough. In Mode 2 knowledge production unrestrained competition can have the effect of inhibiting the growth of networks and of discouraging permeability. Managing the delicate transition between environments appropriate for competition and those appropriate to collaboration implies very complex boundary conditions involving different types of institutions that may be globally distributed. Competition policy has to become competition and collaboration policy, dynamically conceived; not in terms of setting the stage for a zero-sum game, but as creating the environment in which diverse forms of behaviour and organisation can flourish.

The policy has implications on the sensitive problem of international competition and international strategies of collaboration. Far-sighted governments will best pursue their own national interests, not by seeking to develop self-contained national science policies, but by encouraging the growth of international networks and permeability. Success will be determined largely by the ability to extract economic value out of international collaboration. It need not be a predatory act because it is not a zero-sum game.

The new policy will also have to confront a potential imbalance between volatility and permanence of institutions. It may seem that much of what we have said until now will generate only micro-instability. But self-organising systems also produce eigenvalues; that is, regions of macro-stability. Rather than preserving short-term micro-stability by, say, supporting specific firms or sectors, innovation policy needs to aim at long-term sustainable economic development. This is achieved by encouraging diversity, promoting experimentation and creativity, facilitating the emergence of open environments for interaction and exchange. Since this policy will be built upon the importance of people and competence in the innovation process the institutions in which people work will have to find a balance between permanence and change. Institutional managers need to shift the balance from existing, stable and continuous forms of organisation to those which are more flexible and temporary. But it is a question of finding a middle ground between rigidity and chaos.

Future Issues

Mode 2, that is distributed knowledge production, is both open-ended and highly locally contingent. Because of that it would be a mistake to try to provide specific answers here to questions which no doubt are very crucial and need to be addressed everywhere. Practical answers to these questions will have to be found and implemented locally. Nevertheless, at the end of this book we want to highlight six future issues and indicate the likely evolution of underlying trends.

1 *What is the future of funding?* Sources of funding will become increasingly diverse. The power of any individual actor to determine the outcome will concomitantly decrease.
2 *What is the future of disciplinary identities and transdisciplinary competencies?* Formerly secondary, largely multidisciplinary, competencies were added on to primary, largely disciplinary, identities. This pattern will have to be abandoned. A portfolio of identities and competencies will have to be managed, none of which need to be pre-eminent.
3 *How will Mode 2 knowledge be appropriated?* In Mode 2 knowledge production and knowledge appropriation converge. The outcomes are likely to be commensurate with the degree of involvement. Only those who take part in knowledge production are likely to share in its appropriation. The boundaries between private and public appropriation will become increasingly porous.
4 *What is the future of national research systems?* They will experience increasing competition from supranational research organisations, transitory networks and multinational private firms. In order to maintain their function in the future they need to increase permeability, and link up with other research partners.
5 *What is the future of science advisory systems in distributed knowledge production?* There will be a further deconcentration of loci of advice and greater diversity in types of advisers. Governments will have to face the fact they can no longer manage outcomes rather than create some of the conditions for desired outcomes.
6 *Is Mode 2 likely to increase world inequalities?* Yes. There will be an increase of world inequalities in terms of access to and use of the results of scientific and technological activity. Even if Mode 2

knowledge production is more globally dispersed, its economic benefits will be disproportionately reappropriated by rich countries and those who are able to participate.

References

Bush, V. (1946) *Endless Horizons*. Washington, DC: Public Affairs Press.
OECD (1971) *Science Growth and Society*. Brooks Report. OECD.
The Rothschild Report (1971) *The Organisation and Management of Government Research and Development*. Cmnd. 4814. London: HMSO.
Weinberg, A.M. (1963) 'Criteria for scientific choice', *Minerva* 1: 159–71.

Glossary

Codified knowledge: Knowledge which need not be exclusively theoretical but needs to be systematic enough to be written down and stored. As such, it is available to anyone who knows where to look.

Context of application: Problem solving and the generation of knowledge organised around a particular application. Not merely applied research or development. Includes the milieu of interests, institutions and practices which impinge upon the problem to be solved.

Embedded knowledge: Knowledge which cannot move easily across organisational boundaries, its movement is constrained in a given network or set of social relations.

Globalisation: The transformation of national economies into a single international economy.

Heterogeneity: In Mode 2 knowledge production refers to the bringing of multiple skills and experiences to bear on any particular problem. Involves multiple sites, linkages and the differentiation at sites of knowledge production.

Hybrid fora: The meeting point of a range of diverse actors, frequently in public controversies. Hybrid fora can act as new markets for knowledge and expertise.

Knowledge industries: Industries in which knowledge itself is the commodity traded.

Massification: The growth and development of mass higher education.

Migratory knowledge: Knowledge which is mobile and can move rapidly across organisational boundaries.

Mode 1: The complex of ideas, methods, values and norms that has grown up to control the diffusion of the Newtonian model of science to more and more fields of enquiry and ensure its compliance with what is considered sound scientific practice.

Mode 2: Knowledge production carried out in the *context of application* and marked by its: *transdisciplinarity*; *heterogeneity*; organisational heterarchy and transience; social accountability and *reflexivity*; and quality control which emphasises context- and use-dependence. Results from the parallel expansion of knowledge producers and users in society.

Model of increasing density of communication: The increase in communication density at three levels: communication between science and society; communication among scientific practitioners; communication with entities of the physical and social world.

Pluralisation of the elite function: The process by which multi-institutional units or networks are created which qualify as a distributed 'centre' of excellence. Pluralisation occurs as it becomes increasingly difficult for single institutions to qualify as centres of excellence across the whole range of research inputs needed in Mode 2 knowledge production.

Reflexivity: Reflection on the values implied in human aspirations and projects. The process by which individuals involved in knowledge production try to operate from the standpoint of all the actors involved.

Social distribution of knowledge: The diffusion of knowledge production and different *contexts of application* or use over a wide range of potential sites.

Tacit knowledge: Knowledge not available as a text and which may conveniently be regarded as residing in the heads of those working on a particular transformation process, or to be embodied in a particular organisational context.

Technology transfer: The transmission of knowledge from universities to industry. The term **technology interchange** is also used to reflect the interactive nature of this process.

Transdisciplinarity: Knowledge which emerges from a particular *context of application* with its own distinct theoretical structures, research methods and modes of practice but which may not be locatable on the prevailing disciplinary map.

Further Reading

Abramovitz, A. (1986) 'Catching up, forging ahead and falling behind', *Journal of Economic History*, 46(2): 386–406.

Adler, E. (1987) *The Power of Ideology: The Quest for Technological Autonomy in Argentina and Brazil*. Berkeley: University of California Press.

Albrow, M. and King, E. (eds) (1990) *Globalisation, Knowledge and Society*. Special issue of *International Sociology*. London: Sage.

Blume, S. (1992) *Insight and Industry: On the Dynamics of Technological Change in Medicine*. Cambridge, MA: The MIT Press.

Bordieu, P. (1988) *Homo Academicus*. Cambridge: Polity Press in association with Basil Blackwell.

Callon, M., Law, J. and Rip, A. (1986) *Mapping the Dynamics of Science and Technology*. Basingstoke and London: Macmillan.

Clark, N. (1987) 'Similarities and differences between scientific and technological paradigms', *Futures*, 19 (1): 26–42.

Cozzens, S.E. (1990) 'Autonomy and Power in Science', in S.E. Cozzens, and T.F. Gieryn (eds), *Theories of Science in Society*. Indiana: University of Indiana Press.

Crook, S., Pakulski, J. and Waters, M. (1992) *Postmodernization: Change in Advanced Society*. London: Sage.

David, P. (1992) *Knowledge, Property and the System Dynamics of Technological Change*. Paper prepared for the World Bank Annual Conference on Development Economics, Washington, April–May 1992.

Dobuzinskis, L. (1992) 'Modernist and postmodernist metaphors of the policy process: control and stability vs. chaos and reflexive understanding', *Policy Sciences*, 25: 355–80.

Dosi, G. (1982) 'Technological paradigms and technological trajectories', *Research Policy*, 11: 147–62.

Dupré, J. (1993) *The Disorder of Things: Metaphysical Foundations of the Disunity of Science*. Cambridge, MA: Harvard University Press.

Elzinga, A (1985) 'Research, bureaucracy and the drift of epistemic criteria', in B. Wittrock and A. Elzinga (eds), *The University Research System: The Public Policies of the Home of Scientists*. Stockholm: Almqvist and Wiksell International.

Elzinga, A. (1988) 'The consequences of evaluation for academic research', *Science Studies*, 1: 5–14.

Fenger, P. (1992) 'Research councils: buffers under cross pressures', *Higher Education Management*, 4(2): 245–55.

Freeman, C. (1991) 'Grounds for hope: technology, progress and the quality of life', *Science and Public Policy*, 18 (6): 407–18.

Gibbons, M. and Wittrock, B. (eds) (1985) *Science as a Commodity: Threats to the Open Community of Scholars*. Harlow: Longman.

Goggin, M.L. (ed.) (1986) *Governing Science and Technology in a Democracy*. Knoxville: University of Tennessee Press.

170   The New Production of Knowledge

Gummett, P. (1991) 'The evolution of science and technology policy: a UK perspective', *Science and Public Policy*, 18 (1): 31–7.

Hacking, I. (1985) 'Styles of scientific reasoning', in J. Rajchman and C. West (eds), *Post-Analytic Philosophy*. New York: Columbia University Press.

Henkel, M. (1991) 'The new "evaluative state"', *Public Administration*, 69 (Spring): 121–36.

Jassanoff, S.S. (1987) 'Contested boundaries in policy-relevant science', *Social Studies of Science*, 17: 195–230.

Knorr-Cetina, K.D. (1981) *The Manufacture of Knowledge: An Essay on the Constructivist and Contextual Nature of Science*. Oxford and New York: Pergamon Press.

Latour, B. (1987) *Science in Action: How to Follow Scientists and Engineers Through Society*. Milton Keynes: Open University Press.

Lundvall, B. (ed.) (1992) *National Systems of Innovation: Towards a Theory of Innovation and Interactive Learning*. London: Pinter Publishers.

Maxwell, N. (1992) 'What kind of inquiry can best help us create a good world?', *Science, Technology and Human Values*, 17 (2): 205–27.

Midgley, M. (1989) *Wisdom, Information and Wonder: What is Knowledge For?* London and New York: Routledge.

Miller, H. (1991) 'Academics and their labour process', in C. Smith, D. Knights and H. Willmott (eds), *White-Collar Work: The Non-Manual Labour Process*. London: Macmillan.

Mukerji, C. (1989) *A Fragile Power: Scientists and the State*. Princeton: Princeton University Press.

Narin, F. and Noma, E. (1985) 'Is technology becoming science?', *Scientometrics*, 7 (3–6): 369–81.

Nelkin, D. (1992) *Controversy: The Politics of Technical Decisions*, 3rd edn. Newbury Park: Sage.

Nelson, R. and Wright, G. (1992) 'The rise and fall of American technological leadership: the postwar era in historical perspective', *Journal of Economic Literature*, 30 (December): 1931–64.

Phillips, D. and Vervoorn, A. (1990) 'Current trends in research policy', *Prometheus*, 8(2): 331–44.

Porter, M.E. (1990) *The Competitive Advantage of Nations*. New York: Free Press.

Rip, A. (1988) 'Contextual transformations in contemporary science', in A. Jamison (ed.), *Keeping Science Straight: A Critical Look at the Assessment of Science and Technology*. Department of Theory of Science and Centre for Interdisciplinary Studies, University of Gothenburg, Report No 156.

Ronayne, J. (1984) *Science in Government*. London: Edward Arnold.

Rushing, F. and Brown, C.G. (1986) *National Policies for High Technology Industries: International Comparisons*. Westview Special Studies in Science, Technology and Public Policy.

Schwartzman, S. (1991) *A Space for Science: The Development of the Scientific Community in Brazil*. University Park: Pennsylvania University Press.

Turner, S.P. (1990) 'Forms of Patronage', in S.W. Cozzens and T.F. Gieryn (eds), *Theories of Science in Society*. Indiana: University of Indiana Press.

Webster, A. (1991) *Science, Technology and Society*. London and Basingstoke: Macmillan.

Wilkie, T. (1991) *British Science and Politics Since 1945*. Oxford: Blackwell.

Yearley, S. (1988) *Science, Technology and Social Change*. London: Unwin Hyman.

Ziman, J. (1994) *Prometheus Bound: Science in a Dynamic Steady State*. Cambridge: Cambridge University Press.

Index